W9-CHQ-980

CONTENTS

PREFACE

The Key Facts series is designed to give a clear view of each subject. This will be useful to students when tackling new topics and is invaluable as a revision aid. Most chapters open with an outline in diagram form of the points covered in that chapter. The points are then developed in list form to make learning easier. Supporting cases are given throughout by name, and for some complex areas the facts of cases are given to reinforce the point being made.

The topics covered for Land Law are suitable for students studying on a variety of courses, especially first year degree and foundation courses in law. The book also covers topics required for AS examinations.

This is the second edition of Key Facts Land Law. It takes into account any changes that arise as a result of the passing of the Land Registration Act 2002.

The law is as I believe it to be on 1st August 2003.

CHAPTER 1

LAND

Landowner has rights in:

i) airspace (what is reasonable);
ii) minerals (except gold, silver, oil petroleum);
iii) articles in/on the ground (may depend on degree of control exercised by landowner).

Fixtures:

- Items fixed for the improvement and enjoyment of land;
- not chattels.

LAND

Definition

s205(1)(ix) LPA 1925

Real and personal property

Real property:
i) real actions;
ii) gives proprietary rights;
iii) divided into corporeal hereditaments and incorporeal hereditaments.

Personal property:
i) personal actions only;
ii) choice either damages or return item.

Legal and equitable rights

- Legal: enforceable against the whole world.
- Equitable: enforceable against those with notice of these rights.

Notice:

- Actual
- Imputed
- Constructive

1.1 THE SIGNIFICANCE OF LAND

1. Land law essentially deals with the legal relationship between land and the owner of that land.
2. Many different persons can make competing claims to different interests in respect of the same piece of land.
3. The interests of owners of neighbouring land often affect the rights of a landowner, so land should not be seen in isolation.
4. This becomes more significant as more land is taken into residential ownership.
5. Ownership of land therefore comprises not only rights one may have over one's own land, but also rights one may have over a neighbour's land, either to use their land in a particular way or to prevent a particular use they may wish to make of the land.

1.2 THE DEFINITION OF LAND

'Whoever owns the soil owns everything up to the heavens and down to the depths of the earth'.

Definition
s205(1)(ix) Law of Property Act
'Land of any tenure, and mines and minerals, whether or not held apart from the surface, buildings or parts of buildings (whether the division is horizontal, vertical or made in any other way) and other corporeal hereditaments and incorporeal hereditaments...'

— Land —

The landowner has rights to airspace above the land (what is reasonable for the enjoyment of the land) – *Kelsen v Imperial Tobacco* (1957); *Bernstein v Skyviews and General Ltd* (1978)

Articles found in or attached to the land
- Articles found in the land generally belong to the landowner – *Elwes v Briggs Gas Co* (1886); *Waverley BC v Fletcher* (1996).
- Articles found on the land depend on the degree of control over the land – *Parker v British Airways Board* (1982).
- The greater the degree of control the more likely the article belongs to the landowner.

The landowner has rights to mineral deposits, except: gold, silver, coal, oil and natural gas, which all belong to the Crown.

1.3 REAL AND PERSONAL PROPERTY

1. Property is divided into real and personal property.
2. Real property mainly comprises land and is property that can be recovered by a real action, which allows the claimant to recover the property itself.
3. Personal property is property that can only be recovered by a personal action, which allows the defendant a choice between returning the item or paying a sum in damages.
4. Historically, leaseholds were treated as personal property and could be recovered only by personal action, i.e. the claimant might have to be satisfied with damages only.
5. Today the important issue is whether rights over land are personal or proprietary.
6. A proprietary right is a right in the land itself which will even bind a third party purchaser.
7. A lease is now defined as a proprietary right in land.
8. A personal right is a right that is purely personal and cannot bind a third party, e.g. a bare licence which only gives someone the right to remain on the land until the licence is revoked by the licensor.

1.3.1 Real property

1. This can be subdivided into incorporeal and corporeal hereditaments.
2. Hereditaments are rights that can be inherited and so can pass under a will or an intestacy.
3. Corporeal hereditaments are physical objects, e.g. land and anything attached to it, such as buildings, trees and minerals.
4. Incorporeal hereditaments are rights in land that are not physical things, e.g. easements and profits.

1.4 LEGAL AND EQUITABLE RIGHTS

1. Historically:
   - legal rights were enforceable only in the common law courts of the King;
   - equitable rights were enforceable by the King's Chancellor in the Court of Chancery, but only at his discretion.
2. Today, legal rights are distinguished from equitable rights in land because only the owner of a legal estate can deal with the estate at law, and the owner of the equitable estate only has rights in equity.
3. However, in certain circumstances the purchaser may take the estate subject to an equitable estate.
4. Apart from the two legal estates arising under s1(1) LPA 1925 there are lesser interests that are enforceable at law, called legal interests, which are listed under s1(2) LPA 1925, e.g. easements, rentcharges and legal mortgages.
5. Any right that can exist 'at law' may give rise to a legal right, but only if certain statutory requirements are met. Legal rights in land must generally be created and conveyed by deed LPA 1925 s52(1).
6. Any right that does not qualify as a right in law must necessarily exist in equity LPA 1925 s1(3). These include:
   - traditional forms of equitable interest, such as the rights of a beneficiary under a trust;
   - interests that cannot exist at law because some formality has not been complied with;
   - equitable interests under contracts to create legal estates or interests.
7. The main difference lies in the enforceability of these rights against third parties:
   - legal rights are enforceable against the whole world;
   - equitable rights are only enforceable against third parties who have notice of these rights, whether through registration or occasionally because they have actual notice.

1.5 THE DOCTRINE OF NOTICE AND THE 1925 LEGISLATION

> Before 1925 the purchaser of land bought the land subject to an equitable estate if they had notice of the estate. Notice could be actual, constructive or imputed.

A purchaser had **actual notice** if he actually knew of rights affecting the land because he had been told of the rights or he had found out for himself.	A purchaser had **constructive notice** if he would have been aware of the estate if he had checked for himself.	A purchaser would have **imputed notice** if his legal advisors or agents had made investigations. The purchaser should always visit the property because he may still be bound by rights that can only be discovered by physically inspecting the property (*Kingsnorth Trust v Tizard* (1986)).

1.6 FIXTURES

1. When does a chattel become a fixture? *Quinquid plantatur solo, solo cedit* – 'whatever is attached to the soil becomes part of it.'
2. Has the chattel become attached to the land?
   - Chattels fixed to land. Consider:
     - i) the degree of annexation;
     - ii) the object of annexation (*Leigh v Taylor* (1902), *D'Eyncourt v Gregory* (1866), *Berkeley v Poulett* (1976));
     - iii) Was the chattel fixed to the land to improve the land? (fixture)
     - iv) Was the chattel fixed to the land for the use and enjoyment of the chattel? (chattel)
   - Chattels resting on the land. Consider: Were they intended to become part of the land? (fixture) (*Hamp v Bygrave* (1982), *Berkeley v Poulet* (1976), *Elitestone Ltd v Morris* (1997).)

CHAPTER 2
ESTATES AND INTERESTS IN LAND

Legal estates before 1925   **Fee simple**   **Fee tail**   **Life estate**

Legal estates after 1925 (reduced to two)
Fee simple:
● inheritable.
Absolute in possession:
● no limits on ownership;
● immediate enjoyment.
● term of years absolute.

Legal interests after 1925:
● easements;
● rent charges;
● legal mortgages;
● other interests;
● right of re-entry.

Equitable interests:
● interests of a beneficiary under a trust;
● interests under a contract to create legal estates or interests;
● interests which are improperly created;
● interests which become equitable as a result of statutory reform.

2.1 THE DOCTRINE OF ESTATES

1. After 1066 all land was held to be owned by the King, and his subjects were then granted rights in that land.
2. An estate in land was a right of any landowner to enjoy the land as owner for a particular period of time.

3. Before 1925 there were a number of freehold estates in land:
- fee simple – very close to full ownership of land and could continue through successors (*Walsingham's Case* (1573) 'he who has a fee simple in land has a time in the land without end, or the land for time without end');
- fee tail – this lasted as long as the original grantee or his direct descendants were alive;
- life estate – this lasted as long as the life in question.

2.2 Estates in land after 1925

1. After 1925 the number of legal estates in land was reduced to two:
- an estate in fee simple absolute in possession (the freehold estate);
- an estate for a term of years absolute (the leasehold estate), s1(1) Law of Property Act 1925.

2.2.1 The fee simple absolute in possession

1. **Fee Simple** means freehold ownership giving the right for the property to be inherited on death.
2. **Absolute** suggests there are no limits on ownership, e.g. a condition that ownership will cease if X joins the Tory party.
3. **In possession** suggests immediate entitlement to occupation and enjoyment of the land. No one else has a prior claim.
4. A gift of a fee simple subject to a condition, e.g. provided that he becomes a lawyer, will take effect as a conditional fee simple and will be a legal estate in land.
5. A gift of a fee simple that will only last until a determining event occurs will be a determinable fee simple and will take effect in equity only.

2.2.2 Term of years absolute

1. This is a leasehold estate and, unlike the freehold estate, is of limited duration.
2. It must have a fixed and certain maximum duration (*Lace v Chantler* (1944)).
3. A sublease can be created out of the term of years absolute, but this must be a term less than the leasehold, e.g. on a lease for five years, a sublease of four years and eleven months will be valid but a sublease of five years, or five years and a day, will be invalid.

2.2.3 Legal interests

1. Apart from the two legal estates there are lesser rights which can be created at law.
2. These include:
   - an easement, right, or privilege in or over land, for an interest equivalent to an estate in fee simple absolute in possession, or a term of years absolute, s1(2)(a) LPA 1925;
   - a rentcharge in possession (this obliges the purchaser of land to pay money to a named person every year after purchase of a plot of land), s1(2)(b);
   - a charge by way of legal mortgage, s1(2)(c);
   - other similar charge on land not created by an instrument (of very little importance today), s1(2)(d);
   - rights of re-entry exercisable over a legal term of years absolute (this is the right reserved to the owner of the rentcharge to enter the land if the owner of the estate fails to pay the sum due), s1(2)(e).

2.3 EQUITABLE INTERESTS

1. Any interest that does not qualify as a legal interest must be an equitable interest, s1(3) LPA 1925.

2. They fall into several different categories:
   - **the interests of a beneficiary under a trust** – the trustee owns the legal estate and the beneficiary owns the equitable estate;
   - **interests under contract to create legal estates or interests** – the purchaser is treated as owning an equitable estate from the date the contracts are exchanged;
   - **interests that are improperly created** – a deed must be used to convey an interest in land and it must be signed, witnessed and delivered;
   - **interests that become equitable as the result of statutory reform** – any interest that is not within s1(1) or s1(2) LPA 1925, e.g. life estates will only exist in equity.

2.4 OVERREACHING

1. Overreaching is a process whereby the rights of beneficiaries under a trust have their rights taken from the trust property, and attached instead to the capital money.
2. Once overreached the purchaser takes the estate free from all the beneficiary's rights, even if he had actual notice of them (*City of London Building Society v Flegg* (1988)).
3. The overreaching provisions will only protect the purchaser if the capital money is paid to no fewer than two trustees, or to a trust corporation (*Williams & Glyns Bank Ltd v Boland* (1981)).
4. Some interests can never be overreached, e.g. restrictive covenants and estate contracts.

2.5 LEASES AND LICENCES

1. The law distinguishes between a lease and a licence.
2. The significance of the distinction is that a lease will give the tenant a proprietary estate in land, but the licence will only give the licensee a contractual right (*Ashburn Anstalt v Arnold* (1989)).

3. The rights of the licensee are personal only and can never bind a third party purchaser unless they expressly buy subject to those rights.

4. A licensee cannot claim protection from legislation passed to protect tenants, e.g. The Rent Act 1977 or the Housing Act 1988.

5. The agreements for leases and tenancies often appear similar in content.

6. The main distinguishing feature is whether the agreement gives the occupier exclusive possession of the premises.

CHAPTER 3
THE LAND CHARGES ACT 1925

Principles:
  i) Involves investigation of title deeds.
  ii) Sale and other transactions will trigger registration of title.
  iii) Registration of charges in name of owner under Land Charges Act.
  iv) Registration gives notice to whole world.
  v) Failure to register renders the right void against a purchase.

Equitable rights in unregistered land:
  ● estate contracts;
  ● equitable charges;
  ● equitable easements and profits *à prendre*;
  ● restrictive covenants;
  ● beneficial interests under a trust.

UNREGISTERED CONVEYANCING

Registration of charges:
  ● Six classes of land charge.
  ● Effects of non-registration depends on class of land charge.
  ● Class C(iv), D(i), (ii) and (iii) must be sale to purchaser of a legal estate for money or money's worth.

3.1 REASONS FOR THE 1925 LEGISLATION

1. The 1925 legislation introduced many long overdue reforms to land law.
2. The main aims were to:
   ● simplify conveyancing;

- reduce the number of legal estates in land to two;
- provide a system to secure rights for those people owning equitable rights;
- extend the system of registration of land charges in unregistered land;
- extend the system of registration of title;
- abolish outdated rules and practices.

3.2 PRINCIPLES OF UNREGISTERED CONVEYANCING

1. Although most titles of property in England and Wales are registered, or must be registered when a transaction takes place which triggers first registration, there remain some unregistered titles.
2. The purchase of an unregistered title involved investigation of the title deeds on each transaction.
3. Today, sale of an unregistered property will take place under the old rules, but first registration at the Land Registry must then follow.
4. These unregistered titles are subject to the Land Charges Act 1972 (formerly the LCA 1925).
5. Registration of charges must be made under the name of the owner of the property rather than the name or number of the property (LCA 1972 s3).
6. Registration is deemed to give notice to the whole world (s198 LPA 1925).
7. Failure to register renders the right ineffective against a purchaser, even if they have actual notice of the right (*Midland Bank Trust Co Ltd v Green* (1981)).
8. There remain a small number of rights in unregistered land that are subject to the doctrine of the *bona fide* purchaser for value without notice:
    - the most important of these are the equitable interests of a beneficiary under a trust of land where the legal title has been conveyed by a sole trustee of land (*Kingsnorth Trust v Tizard* (1986));

- also those rights based on proprietary estoppel (*ER Ives Investment Ltd v High* (1967)).

3.3 EQUITABLE RIGHTS IN UNREGISTERED LAND

1. These include, as in the case of registered land, different categories of rights.
2. Rights that are inherently equitable, such as:
   - estate contracts;
   - equitable charges;
   - equitable easements and profits *à prendre*;
   - restrictive covenants;
   - beneficial interests under a trust of land.

3.4 SYSTEM OF REGISTRATION

1. Rights are registered under classes of land charge.
2. Under the 1972 LCA there are six classes of land charge, A–F (as shown in the diagram on page 14).
3. The effect of non-registration of the charge depends on the class of charge involved.
4. Classes C(iv) and D(i), (ii) and (iii) will still be binding unless there has been a sale to a purchaser of a legal estate for money or money's worth, and the purchaser of a lesser estate will still be bound by these classes of land charge. Need not be full value.
5. A purchaser of an estate will take free of a non-registered charge in the other classes.

3.5 MOVE TOWARDS REGISTRATION OF ALL TITLES

1. The introduction of the Land Registration Act 2002 will result in the gradual phasing out of unregistered charges.
2. Most dispositions of interests in unregistered land will represent a trigger for registration of title.

3.4.1 The effect of registration or non-registration of interests in land with unregistered title

Unregistered Land:

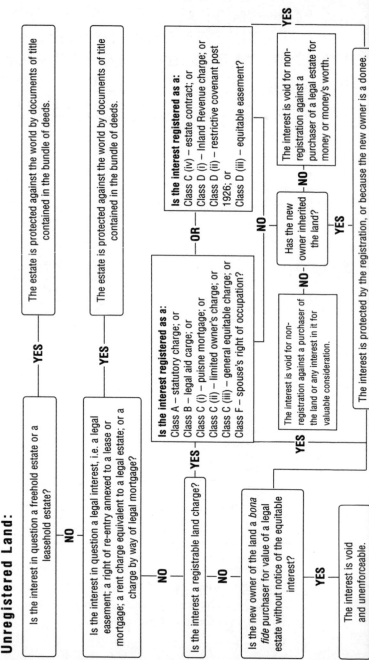

Is the interest in question a freehold estate or a leasehold estate?

YES — The estate is protected against the world by documents of title contained in the bundle of deeds.

NO

Is the interest in question a legal interest, i.e. a legal easement; a right of re-entry annexed to a lease or mortgage; a rent charge equivalent to a legal estate; or a charge by way of legal mortgage?

YES — The estate is protected against the world by documents of title contained in the bundle of deeds.

NO

Is the interest a registrable land charge?

YES —

Is the interest registered as a:
Class A – statutory charge; or
Class B – legal aid carge; or
Class C (i) – puisne mortgage; or
Class C (ii) – limited owner's charge; or
Class C (iii) – general equitable charge; or
Class F – spouse's right of occupation?

OR

Is the interest registered as a:
Class C (iv) – estate contract; or
Class D (i) – Inland Revenue charge; or
Class D (ii) – restrictive covenant post 1926; or
Class D (iii) – equitable easement?

The interest is void for non-registration against a purchaser of the land or any interest in it for valuable consideration.

The interest is void for non-registration against a purchaser of a legal estate for money or money's worth.

NO

Is the new owner of the land a *bona fide* purchaser for value of a legal estate without notice of the equitable interest?

YES →

Has the new owner inherited the land?

NO

YES

The interest is protected by the registration, or because the new owner is a donee.

YES

The interest is void and unenforceable.

CHAPTER 4

REGISTRATION OF TITLE

The three registers:
- the property register;
- the charges register;
- the proprietorship register.

Categories of interests:
- registrable interests;
- registered charges;
- minor interests;
- overriding interests.

RIGHTS IN REGISTERED LAND

Rectification and indemnity:
Schedule 4
i) para (1), alteration of the register
  a) involves the correction of a mistake
  b) prejudicially affects the title of the registered proprietor
ii) para (2)
  a) correcting a mistake
  b) bringing the register up to date, or
  c) giving effect to any estate, right or interest excepted from the effect of registration
iii) para (3)
  in addition to power under para (2) power to remove superfluous entries
iv) para (8) indemnity payable for
  a) loss suffered through rectification
  b) loss through a mistake involving rectification.

Minor interests
Equitable interests that are neither registrable estates/charges nor overriding.
Protected by:
i) notice;
ii) restriction;
iii) LRA 2002 removed cautions and inhibitions.

Overriding interests
LRA 2002 reduces the number of overriding interests
Status depends on whether first/subsequent registration
Interests that are NOT overriding under the 2002 Act
Leases less than 7 years
Equitable easements
Rights under the Limitation Act 1980

Rights overriding first registration:
Short leases (less than 7 years)
Rights of persons in actual occupation
Legal easements and profits

4.1 FEATURES OF REGISTRATION OF TITLE

1. The system of registration of title introduced by the Land Registration Act 1925 reflects three principles:
   - i) the 'mirror principle';
   - ii) the 'insurance principle';
   - iii) the 'curtain principle'.
2. Under the 'mirror principle' it is held that the register is an accurate and conclusive reflection of relevant interests affecting the land in question.
3. Under the 'insurance principle' the accuracy of the register is guaranteed and, if the register is found to be inaccurate, persons affected by rectification/non-rectification are entitled to be indemnified.
4. Under the 'curtain principle' the purchaser of land is not concerned with matters behind the entries on the register, e.g. trusts affecting the land should not be entered on the register.

4.2 THE LAND REGISTRY

1. The Land Registry consists of three registers.

The property register This describes the property and will refer to a filed plan prepared from an ordnance survey map.	**The charges register** This section shows details of any incumbrances registered against the estate, e.g. easements, restrictive covenants.

The proprietorship register
This shows the name and address of the registered proprietor of the relevant title, the date of registration and the nature of the title, e.g. absolute, good leasehold, qualified or possessory.

2. Since 1988 the general public has had access to the register on payment of a fee. Previously access was only with the permission of the registered proprietor of the land.

4.3 CLASSIFICATION OF INTERESTS IN REGISTERED LAND

1. In registered land there are four categories of interests:
   a) registrable interests;
   b) registered charges;
   c) minor interests;
   d) overriding interests.
2. Registrable interests are rights in land that are capable of substantive registration: the fee simple absolute in possession and the term of years absolute in possession although this is not registrable unless it exceeds 7 years.
3. Although registration of title is now compulsory there remain substantial numbers of titles that are not yet registered.
4. There is no requirement to register title unless there is a disposition affecting the title, e.g. a conveyance for value.
5. If there is no disposition within the meaning of the act then registration is not necessary. If property is owned by a corporate body then property may not change hands for considerable periods of time. As an incentive to landowners to bring property within the system of registration there is a reduction in fees for anyone who registers their property voluntarily.

4.3.1 Events that trigger first registration

1. s4(1) lists the events which trigger compulsory registration.
2. Transfers of a qualifying estate either for valuable consideration or by way of gift or in pursuance of an order of any court or by means of an assent.
3. Leases granted for more than 7 years.
4. First legal mortgages of a qualifying estate.
5. Grant of a 'right to buy' under the Housing Act 1985.
6. s5 allows the Lord Chancellor by order to add new events that will trigger compulsory registration.

4.3.2 First registration of title

1. When property with unregistered title changes hands then there must be first registration of title. This can take several forms:
   - Absolute freehold title – this is the most frequently awarded class of title and is the most reliable. The owner has all the rights of a fee simple absolute owner subject to rights appearing on the register and overriding interests.
   - Possessory freehold title – an applicant will get a mere possessory title if they cannot produce sufficient documentary evidence of title. The effect is such that they remain subject to all adverse interests existing at the date of registration.
   - Qualified freehold title – this is extremely rare and is granted where the applicant has some defect in his title so that registration takes subject to that defect.
2. An application for first registration must be made within two months of a disposition triggering the requirement for first registration.
3. Failure to register has drastic effects. The disposition becomes statutorily void for the purposes of transferring, granting or creating a legal estate. The title then takes effect in equity only. The title reverts back to the vendor who holds it on bare trust for the transferee.
4. After first registration all later transfers must be recorded in the register to become effective at law. Until registration the vendor holds as trustee and the purchaser has only an equitable estate in the property. There is no time limit for registration, but delay risks the possibility of dealings in the property by the vendor.

4.4 DEFINITION OF MINOR INTERESTS

1. All interests in registered land which are neither registrable estates/charges nor overriding interests take effect merely in equity and are known as minor interests.

2. Minor interests can be protected by entry on the relevant register of title of either a notice or a restriction.

3. Once a minor interest has been protected in this way, subsequent transferees of the registered freehold or leasehold estate will be bound by such interests.

4. Failure to register on the relevant register of title makes the interest ineffective against a purchaser for value of any subsequent registered disposition, and it is irrelevant that the purchaser knows about the interest.

5. The purchaser will normally check the register prior to completion to see if there are any rights affecting the vendor's land.

6. Where there are two or more minor interests that have been duly protected by entries on the same title, the priority of the interests is governed by their dates of creation and not by the date of registration.

4.4.1 Protection of minor interests

Notice
- A notice could not be registered unless the relevant land certificate was produced and it required the co-operation of the registered proprietor.
- It did not normally constitute a hostile form of entry.

Caution
- Almost all forms of minor interest could be protected by the entry of a 'caution against dealing' in the Proprietorship Register of an already registered title.
- Cautions were generally used in hostile situations. They could effect the registered proprietor's ability to dispose of the estate.
- The proprietor could challenge the entry.

OLD METHOD OF PROTECTION OF MINOR INTERESTS

Inhibition
- An inhibition entered on the proprietorship register of the relevant title prevented any registered dealing in the land.
- Usually used where the land certificate had been stolen from the registered proprietor or where a bankruptcy order had been made in respect of a registered proprietor.

Restriction
This had the effect of limiting the proprietor's power to dispose of the property, e.g. in a trust of land there may have been a restriction on dealing with a sole trustee.

4.4.2 New methods of protection of minor interests

The LRA 2002 allows for only two forms of entry **notice** and **restriction**.

1. Notices
- entry of a notice does not necessarily mean that the interest is valid but it will be protected against a purchaser of the registered estate for valuable consideration;
- some interests cannot be protected by notice e.g. interests under a trust of land (should be protected by restriction), a lease for not more than three years and restrictive covenants in leases;
- normally the notice will be agreed between the parties;
- a unilateral notice may be entered without the consent of the registered proprietor although they have the opportunity to object. These replace cautions against dealing.

2. Restrictions
- these literally 'restrict' any dealings with the registered estate or charge;
- under the 2002 Act they replace inhibitions and old restrictions;
- restrictions may be entered in respect of a specific type of disposition or all dispositions;
- a restriction must be entered where two or more people are registered as proprietor to ensure that interests capable of being overreached are overreached;
- a restriction must not be used to protect an interest which is capable of protection by notice;
- the registered proprietor need not be asked first but must be informed of their existence.

3. Inhibitions
- These have now been abolished by the LRA 2002.
- They are replaced by restrictions.
- They will remain on the register during the transitional arrangements.

4. Cautions
- A caution is a protective entry which appeared on the proprietorship register.
- Cautions against interests on subsequent registration have been abolished by the LRA 2002.
- Existing cautions remain valid after the act comes into force.
- Cautions can still be entered against first registration.
- These cautions will be held in a new cautions register.
- The effect of these cautions is such that the cautioner will be notified of any application to register the property.

4.4.3 Effect of registration of minor interests

1. The knowledge of the transferee of any unregistered interest will generally be irrelevant. 'It is vital to the working of the Land Registration system that notice of something which is not on the register should not affect a transferee unless it is an overriding interest' (*Strand Securities v Caswell* (1965)).
2. Where a disposition is made without valuable consideration then unprotected minor interests remain binding on the transferee.
3. The transferee of a registered title who is guilty of fraud may never disclaim a minor interest merely on the ground that it was not entered on the register at the date of his own registration as proprietor.
4. Fraud is not strictly defined but it is usually associated with some personal dishonesty. It does not normally include a purchaser who takes advantage of another's failure to register interests on the register.
5. So, mere knowledge of the existence of unprotected rights does not suggest fraud on the part of the disponee of the registered title (*De Lusignan v Johnson* (1973)).
6. The law will treat a transferee in bad faith differently, and he/she cannot rely on the statutory immunity (*Peffer v Rigg* (1977)). Graham J held that unprotected minor interests are

rendered statutorily ineffective only as against a purchaser 'in good faith'. However, this case has not been widely followed.

7. If the transfer is made expressly subject to unprotected rights then a constructive trust may be generated. This is because the parties to the transfer had the express object of conferring new rights which they would not have otherwise have enjoyed (*Lyus v Prowsa Developments Ltd* (1982)).

8. New rights will only be conferred where the undertaking is an express stipulation or other factors make it unconscionable to deny the right, e.g. there has been a reduction in purchase price (*Ashburn Anstalt v Arnold* (1989)).

4.4.4 Priority between minor interests

1. Where two or more minor interests have been entered on the register their priority is generally governed by their respective dates of creation (*Barclays Bank v Taylor* (1974)).

2. Priority remains with the interest that is created earlier, even if it is entered on the register after the registration of the later interest.

3. Recently, it has been held that priority may be displaced where there is clear evidence of fraud on behalf of the owner of the earlier interest (*Freeguard v Royal Bank of Scotland PLC* (2000)).

4.5 OVERRIDING INTERESTS

4.5.1 Definition

S3 (xvi) Land Registration Act 1925: 'all the incumbrances, interests, rights and powers not entered on the register but subject to which registered dispositions are by the Act to take effect...'

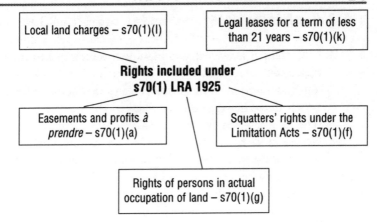

4.5.2 The nature of an overriding interest

1. Overriding interests (with the exception of easements) never appear on the register of title.
2. Overriding interests are a mixed category of rights that are simply declared 'overriding' by statute, even though the transferee may have no actual knowledge of their existence.
3. The Law Commission justified their non-registrable existence in 1971 by saying that registration of some interests is either 'unnecessary, impracticable or undesirable'.
4. These interests can usually be discovered by inspecting the land and making inquiries of the vendor.
5. Easements are an exception to the rule that overriding interests never appear on the register. Although they are rights capable of registration both in law and in equity, under s70(1)(a) they could also constitute overriding interests (*Celsteel Ltd v Alton House Holdings Ltd* (1985)).
6. The most significant overriding rights are the rights of every person in actual occupation of the land at the relevant time.
7. Occupation without rights in the land does not constitute an overriding interest. It is argued that the occupation will transform the rights into overriding interests in the same way that the entry of a notice will transform a minor interest into an enforceable interest but without rights this cannot happen.

4.5.3 Overriding interests under the LRA 2002

1. Overriding interests cause uncertainty because they do not appear on the register.
2. The LRA aims to create an electronic system of conveyancing which allows investigation on line.
3. The LRA achieves this in relation to overriding interests in the following ways:
   a) reducing the scope of some overriding interests;
   b) providing for the eventual abolition of others;
   c) requiring people applying for some registrations to provide information about unregistered interests so that they can be noted on the register;
   d) once an interest has been noted then it loses its overriding status.
5. The Act distinguishes between interests which override first registration (schedule one) and interests which override second and subsequent registration (schedule three).
6. Certain interests differ between the two schedules e.g. short leases under seven years override under the 2002 Act but leases under 21 years were overriding under the 1925 Act.
7. Some interests will retain overriding status indefinitely e.g. a customary right, a public right, a local land charge.
8. Some interests will lose their overriding status after 10 years e.g. a franchise, a manorial right. These will need to be protected before 13th October 2013.
9. Anyone applying for first registration or to register a registrable disposition must give the registrar information about overriding rights affecting their property.

4.5.4 Rights of persons in actual occupation

1. Under the 1925 Act anyone with a proprietary right in property and also in actual occupation could claim an overriding interest, e.g. an estate contract, an option to purchase a freehold interest, an equitable interest under a trust of land.

2. Rights incapable of qualifying as overriding rights:
   - Matrimonial rights under the Family Law Act 1996 are only binding if protected on the register. The FLA expressly excludes them from existing as overriding interests.
   - Bare licences do not constitute qualifying interests (*Strand Securities v Caswell* (1965)).
   - Contractual licences do not constitute qualifying interests (*Ashburn Anstalt v Arnold* (1989)).
3. It was assumed that there would be no overlap between minor interests and overriding interests.
4. However, it was held by the House of Lords in *Williams & Glyn's Bank v Boland* in 1981 that where an interest was unprotected by entry on the register it could still take effect as an overriding interest under s70(1)(g).
5. The practical effect of an overriding interest is that it will be capable of binding a third party purchaser of the land.
6. If the overriding interest is overreached because the purchase money is paid to two trustees it will not be binding on the third party purchaser (*City of London Building Society v Flegg* (1988)).

4.5.5 The meaning of Actual Occupation

1. Actual occupation will vary according to the type of land that is claimed to be occupied. Differing standards of 'actual occupation' might be relevant to an ordinary dwelling house fit for habitation and a semi-derelict property (*Lloyd's Bank v Rosset* (1989)).
2. Permanent residence cannot be claimed in respect of business or agricultural premises.
3. There is no need to be permanently in occupation provided the claimant is normally present. So a temporary absence will not prevent actual occupation so long as there is evidence of permanent presence. A woman who had left the premises to have a baby in hospital could claim an overriding interest

binding on the purchaser who had purchased her home in her absence (*Chhokar v Chhokar* (1984)).

4. The mere taking of preparatory steps leading to the assumption of actual residential occupation is not sufficient (*Abbey National Building Society v Cann* (1991)).

5. Minor children living with their parents who had beneficial interests in property could not be 'in actual occupation' under s70(1)(g) (*Hypo-Mortgage Services Ltd v Robinson* (1997)).

6. In *Lloyd's Bank v Rosset* (1989) it was held in the Court of Appeal that a wife who was engaged in renovatory work on a semi-derelict house could be in actual occupation both in her own right or through her builders. The House of Lords did not address this issue and rejected her claim to rights on the basis that she did not have a proprietary right.

7. If a person only occupies part of the land the interest is only protected so far as it relates to that part (reverses *Ferrishurst Ltd v Wallcite Ltd* (1999)).

8. Interests belonging to persons receiving rent and profits but not actually occupying the land are no longer protected.

9. On a subsequent registration of property an interest in occupation will not be overriding if it was not apparent on careful inspection of the property and the person to whom the disposition is made does not have knowledge at that time.

4.5.6 The meaning of enquiry

1. Under s70(1)(g) the rights of every person in actual occupation constituted an overriding interest 'save where enquiry is made of such person and the rights are not disclosed'.

2. Any purchaser had to ensure that the person in actual occupation was asked what rights he or she had in the land.

3. If the person in occupation concealed his rights then he was deprived of full protection.

4. The rules concerning 'enquiry' have changed for first registration under the 2002 Act.

5. It is now not necessary to make enquiries of the person in actual occupation on first registration.
6. On subsequent registration an interest will not be protected if inquiry was made of the person claiming it before the disposition took place and he failed to disclose it when he could reasonably have been expected to do so.

4.5.7 Effective date of overriding interests

1. Under the LRA 2002 registrable dispositions are not enforceable until completed by registration at HM Land Registry.
2. The date of registration is deemed to be date of lodging the application for registration.
3. The date for determining the existence of overriding interests is the date of registration of the relevant disposition (*Abbey National Building Society v Cann* (1991)).

4.6 RECTIFICATION AND INDEMNITY

4.6.1 When is rectification available?

1. Rectification of a registered title is not generally available. It can only be allowed under statutory authority.
2. An applicant for rectification must establish one or more of the grounds contained within Land Registration Act 2002 schedule 4 para 2:
   a) correcting a mistake;
   b) bringing the register up to date, or
   c) giving effect to any estate, right or interest excepted from the effect of registration.
   Under schedule 4 para 3, the Registrar can alter the register without a court order on these grounds. He also has power to remove superfluous entries.
3. The award of rectification is not automatic but discretionary.

4. Schedule 8 LRA 2002 allows an indemnity to be paid for loss
suffered by reason of rectification or non-rectification of the
register.

5. No right to an indemnity arises if:
- a registered title is rectified to give effect to a subsisting
  overriding interest because no loss has been suffered by the
  rectification (*Re Chowood's Registered Land* (1933));
- the applicant for indemnity has suffered loss wholly or partly
  in consequence of his own fraud or lack of proper care;
- it would be unjust for the alteration to be made.

4.7 SUMMARY OF CHANGES TO LAND REGISTRATION UNDER THE 2002 ACT

1. The Act extends compulsory registration to include leases
with more than seven years to run.

2. The methods of protecting the interests of third parties over
registered land are reduced to two: notices and restrictions.

3. Mortgages by demise or sub-demise can no longer be granted
over registered land.

4. Overriding interests can only be overriding where it is
unreasonable to expect them to be protected in the register.

5. The number of overriding interests has been reduced.

6. There is a duty to disclose rights on registration of the
property if the right is known to you.

7. The Act paves the way for the formation of a secure electronic
network within which to carry out e-conveyancing.

8. The rules concerning the acquisition of rights by adverse
possession have been changed making it far more difficult to
acquire such rights.

9. Equitable easements are no longer overriding.

10. All legal easements will be overriding on first registration but
only implied legal easements will override on a subsequent
registration.

CHAPTER 5

INFORMAL CREATION OF RIGHTS IN LAND

Definition of a trust

The legal title in property held by trustees for beneficiaries who hold an equitable title.
- Express
- Implied

Resulting trusts
- X contributes purchase money for property in Y's name.
- Can be rebutted by evidence of Presumption of advancement.
- Usually share is proportionate to contributions, but court has discretion to order otherwise.

INFORMAL CREATION OF RIGHTS IN LAND

Proprietary estoppel
- Definition: X assures Y of future rights and Y relies on the assurance and acts to his detriment.
- Court has wide discretion to award remedies.

Constructive trusts
a) The 'express bargain' constuctive trust:
   i) must be some actual agreement, but need not be in writing;
   ii) must be some detrimental reliance.
b) The 'implied bargain' constructive trust:
   i) conduct and mutual dealings;
   ii) proof of detriment very strict;
   iii) never contributions in kind.

5.1 IMPLIED TRUSTS

5.1.1 The definition of a trust

1. A trust allows ownership in property to be split between legal and equitable ownership.

2. The legal title to property is held by one or more persons (the trustee).

3. The beneficiaries are entitled to the equitable title.

4. The trustee holds on behalf of the beneficiaries who take the benefit of the trust.

5. Trusts are split into two categories:
- the express trust based on the declared intentions of the parties; and
- the implied trust, generally based on the presumed intentions of the parties.

5.1.2 The express trust

1. The settlor asks the trustees expressly to hold property on trust for the beneficiaries on the terms named by the settlor.

2. Alternatively, the owner of property could declare himself to be trustee of the land on behalf of X, the beneficiary.

3. The creation of the trust must comply with s53(1)(b) LPA 1925, which requires evidence in writing. Without written evidence the trust is unenforceable.

4. The trustee is under a duty under the common law and the Trustee Acts 1925, 2000, to act in the best interests of the beneficiaries and according to the settlor's instructions.

5. The beneficiaries have the right to compel the trustees to carry out the terms of the trust.

6. If the court finds the trustee to be in breach of his duties then he may be compelled to compensate the trust.

5.1.3 The implied trust

1. In land law today the vast majority of trusts arise by implication.

2. The court will impose an implied trust where it decides to give effect to the presumed intention or informal bargains of the parties.

3. Implied trusts do not require any formalities (LPA 1925 s53(2)). In some cases the courts may find an implied trust where the formalities of an express trust have not been complied with by the parties.

4. There are two types of implied trust:
   - the resulting trust; and
   - the constructive trust.

5.2 RESULTING TRUSTS

5.2.1 Definition of resulting trusts

1. A money contribution towards the purchase of a legal estate in the name of another will create the presumption of a resulting trust.

   For example:
   a) X provides £60,000 for the purchase of Whiteacre in Y's name. Y holds on resulting trust for X.
   b) X and Y provide £60,000 for the purchase of Blackacre in the name of Y. Y holds on resulting trust for X and Y.

2. A resulting trust can arise where the parties are unaware that a trust been imposed.

3. This can be rebutted by evidence that the money was meant as a gift or a loan.

4. In some circumstances the relationship of the parties will allow the presumption of a gift.

5. A gift will be presumed between father and child (*Dyer v Dyer* (1788)) and historically between husband and wife.

6. a) X provides £60,000 for the purchase of Whiteacre in Y's name. Y holds on resulting trust for X
   b) If X is Y's father then the resulting trust will be rebutted and the £60,000 will be presumed to be a gift.

5.2.2 The operation of Resulting Trusts

1. A resulting trust can be easily implied where there is a direct cash contribution to the purchase price (*Cowcher v Cowcher* (1972)).
2. If two or more contribute to the purchase price, then it is presumed that their shares will be proportionate to their contributions.
3. However, this is not always the case and the court can order shares that are not directly proportionate to their contributions (*Midland Bank v Cooke* (1995)). In this case the court held that in spite of a mere 6.4% contribution by Mrs Cooke she was found to have a half share in the property.
4. A contribution can be the exercise of the 'right to buy' under the Housing Act 1985. The share will represent the reduction in purchase price awarded to the qualifying tenant (*Springette v Defoe* (1992)).
5. A resulting trust can arise where contributions take the form of contributions to mortgage repayments after the initial purchase of the property (*Gissing v Gissing* (1971)).
6. It is rare for contributions to the general household expenses to be sufficient to establish a resulting trust: 'the fact that parties live together and do the ordinary domestic tasks is...no indication at all that they...intended to alter the existing property rights of either of them' (*Burns v Burns* (1984)).
7. Contributions to living expenses may be sufficient if there is an express agreement that the expenses are to be regarded as giving rise to a share in the property.

5.3 CONSTRUCTIVE TRUSTS

5.3.1 The definition of constructive trusts

1. The constructive trust covers a variety of situations, but in land law it is imposed largely in situations where 'the trustee has so conducted himself that it would be inequitable to allow

him to deny to the beneficiary a beneficial interest in the land acquired' (Lord Diplock in *Gissing v Gissing* (1971)).

2. Lord Bridge laid down in *Lloyds Bank plc v Rosset* (1991) that there are two situations giving rise to a constructive trust:
   - the express bargain constructive trust:
     i) there must be an agreement or understanding between the legal owners and the non-legal owners to share the equitable interest;
     ii) the non-legal owners relied on that agreement and acted to their detriment.
   - the implied bargain constructive trust:
     i) the court considers the conduct of the parties and from their conduct infers a common intention to share the equitable interest;
     ii) the court must establish that the non-legal owners have made contributions towards the purchase price (must be direct contributions).

3. The non-legal owner acquires an equitable interest in the land under constructive trust.

5.3.2 The 'express bargain constructive trust': the agreement

1. There must be some evidence of an actual agreement between the legal estate owner X to share the property beneficially with Y (Lord Bridge in *Lloyd's Bank v Rosset* (1991)).
2. Unlike resulting trusts (where evidence of intention must be present at the initial purchase) it is possible to find evidence of a constructive trust at any time.
3. There must be clear evidence of an express discussion even if the terms were imprecise in legal terms.
4. If there is evidence of the discussion it can be upheld by a court even if there is no written evidence.
5. The type of rights conferred on Y can range from the equitable estate to a lesser interest, such as an option to purchase.

6. The court will never infer a constructive trust where there is a mere assumption in a family situation that rights will be acquired (*Lloyd's Bank v Rosset* (1991)).
7. The express agreement must be supported by some change in position, which can take any form.

5.3.3 The detrimental reliance

1. Apart from the agreement, there must also be evidence of detrimental reliance.
2. This is a change of position by Y in reliance on the promise by X.
3. The change in position must be connected with the property, e.g. money and time spent on renovating property by Y in the belief that she will acquire a share. In *Eves v Eves* (1975) a woman carrying out repairs, including wielding 14lb sledgehammer in the garden, was awarded a share in the property; but no award for money and time spent on the property out of affection, as in *Burns v Burns* (1984).
4. It will not be detrimental reliance where there has already been payment or compensation for the contribution, e.g. in *Layton v Martin* (1986) where previously paid domestic duties could not be considered as detrimental reliance for a share in the property.

5.3.4 The 'implied bargain constructive trust'

1. This depends on looking at the conduct and mutual dealings of the parties to find evidence of an agreement.
2. According to Lord Bridge in *Lloyd's Bank v Rosset* (1991), proof of detriment under an 'implied bargain' constructive trust must be much stricter than under an 'express bargain' constructive trust.
3. Only direct contributions to the purchase price, either initially or by way of mortgage instalments later, will be sufficient evidence.

4. Contributions in kind, e.g. work on the property or shared household expenses will never be enough.
5. The change of position must strictly be referable to the acquisition of a beneficial interest in the property (*Gissing v Gissing* (1971)).
6. The award of shares in the property will try to reflect what the parties intended. The courts have considerable discretion, e.g. in *Midland Bank plc v Cooke* (1995)(supra), Waite LJ awarded a wife a half share in the property although her actual contribution was restricted to 6.4% of the purchase price.

5.3.5 The future for constructive trusts

1. There are many limitations on the constructive trust and these can work unfairly for the parties.
2. Other jurisdictions have adopted a fairer approach to the constructive trust, recognising the 'remedial constructive trust'.
3. The court has a far greater discretion in these cases and is not restricted to giving effect to the parties' intentions. The court tries to remedy any 'unjust enrichment'.
4. Canada has developed the doctrine in a number of cases, e.g. *Pettkus v Becker* (1980) and *Sorochan v Sorochan* (1986) where a share of the property was awarded based on domestic and household services.
5. This was echoed in New Zealand (*Gillies v Keogh* (1989)).
6. The UK briefly recognised the doctrine in the 1970s (*Cooke v Head* (1972)), but later returned to stricter property principles.
7. Today, there is considerable criticism of the restrictions that this approach imposes, and the Law Commission is currently working on draft proposals for reform of property rights which will cover a range of situations, including rights of unmarried partners.

5.4 PROPRIETARY ESTOPPEL

5.4.1 Definition of estoppel

1. Estoppel operates where X, the owner of land, has expressly given some assurance to Y respecting present or future rights in land, and Y relies on that assurance and acts to his detriment.
2. The definition of estoppel depends on three elements:
   - a representation (or assurance of rights);
   - reliance (or a change of position);
   - detriment (or unconscionable conduct).
3. The most important question to ask is 'whether it would be unconscionable for a party to be permitted to deny that which, unknowingly or knowingly, he has allowed or encouraged another to assume to his detriment' (*Taylor Fashions Ltd v Liverpool Trustees Co Ltd* (1982)).

5.4.2 The representation

1. This must relate to a present or future interest in land of the person making the representation or creating the expectation.
2. It is not, however, necessary to formulate the claim in terms of a specific type of interest, e.g. an equitable estate.
3. Promises must be clear and unequivocal. Claims will be rejected if they are no more than gratuitous promises or are excessively vague.
4. Promises made in respect of gifts under a will are generally unenforceable because the testator can always revoke the will before death.
5. In some circumstances the claim will be upheld where the testator's promises are very clear and are relied on by the claimant over a long period of time. In *Gillett v Holt* (2000), a wealthy farmer promised a farm worker rights in his land over a period of forty years, but changed his will when they had a serious row. The court upheld the claim by the farm worker.

6. A representation can be made by silence. However, mere delay in acting on a trespass or a breach will not confer rights.

5.4.3 Reliance

1. The claimant must show that he has changed his position in reliance on the representation made by the owner of the land. The claimant must have altered his position (*Re Basham* (1986)).
2. There must also be a causal link between the representation and the change of position.
3. The claimant need not have altered his position exclusively in reliance on the representation.
4. The change of position can either be quantified in money terms or in contributions of labour or abandoning a job in order to come and live with or near the representor.
5. Inconvenience or altered lifestyle will not represent a change of position (*Coombes v Smith* (1986)).
6. The burden of proof lies with the claimant to show that the representation has been made and the claimant has altered his position.
7. Once a representation has been made and the claimant has altered his position, giving an inference that he acted in reliance on the promise, then the burden of proof shifts to the landowner to show that there was no reliance on the promise (*Greasley v Cooke* (1980)).

5.4.4 Detriment

1. The representee must be shown to be unconscionably disadvantaged by relying on the representation.
2. In recent cases the courts generally seek proof of both detrimental reliance by the claimant and proof that the landowner is acting unconscionably in seeking to enforce his strict legal rights (*Gillett v Holt* (2000)).
3. Under equitable principles there may be bars to relief, e.g. delay or 'lack of clean hands' will prevent a successful claim.

5.4.5 Nature of the rights arising under Proprietary Estoppel

1. Proprietary Estoppel entitles the claimant to some form of equitable relief.
2. The registrar has allowed the right to be entered on the register.
3. It is also capable of taking effect as an overriding interest.
4. Under s116 Land Registration Act 2002 the right will take effect from the time when the claimant acted to his/her detriment.
5. Once the right takes affect it is capable of binding third parties.

5.4.6 Remedies in estoppel

1. The court must look at the circumstances in each case to decide in what way the equity can be satisfied (*Plimmer v Mayor of Wellington* (1884)).
2. The court has a very wide discretion in remedies it is prepared to award.
3. Estoppel can be used as a sword and a shield, e.g. it can found a cause of action as well as defending a cause of action.

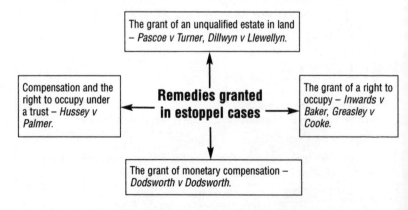

The grant of an unqualified estate in land – *Pascoe v Turner, Dillwyn v Llewellyn.*

Compensation and the right to occupy under a trust – *Hussey v Palmer.*

Remedies granted in estoppel cases

The grant of a right to occupy – *Inwards v Baker, Greasley v Cooke.*

The grant of monetary compensation – *Dodsworth v Dodsworth.*

CHAPTER 6

CO-OWNERSHIP

Types of co-ownership

The joint tenancy
- The rights of survivorship;
- the four unities:
  - i) possession;
  - ii) title; iii) interest; iv) time;
- no share in property.

The tenancy in common
- The right of survivorship does not operate.
- Individual shares.

Joint tenancy or tenancy in common?

a) Any words of severance;
b) any of the four unities absent;
c) unequal contributions;
d) commercial purchase;
e) lessees of business premises;
f) joint mortgagees of property.

Methods of severance

Statute: a) s36(2) written notice.
Common law: b) Joint tenant (acting on his share):
  i) an act operating on a joint tenant's share;
  ii) mutual agreement;
  iii) mutual conduct.
c) Homicide.

Co-ownership of land after 1996

a) All co-owned land held as 'trust of land'.
b) Trustees have power of absolute owner. Must act unanimously. Must consult beneficiaries.
c) Beneficiaries have:
  - right to occupy;
  - right to be consulted;
  - right to require express consents;
  - right to appoint/remove trustees;
  - right to apply for a court order.
d) Equitable rights can be overreached if rights are capable of being overreached, and the conveyance is made by the trustees, and the purchaser pays purchase money to two trustees. Once overreached, rights transfer from land to purchase money.
e) Any person with interest can apply to the court and the court applies certain criteria:
  i) intentions of persons creating the trust;
  ii) purposes of trust;
  iii) welfare of any minor;
  iv) interests of any secured creditor.
f) Different criteria apply where sale made by trustee in bankruptcy.

6.1 TYPES OF CO-OWNERSHIP

1. Co-ownership describes the ownership of land where two or more people have an interest in the same land at the same time.
2. Two different types of co-ownership are recognised today: the joint tenancy and the tenancy in common.
3. Under the joint tenancy, each joint tenant is said to be wholly entitled to the whole of the estate or interest that is the subject of co-ownership.
4. The tenancy in common differs because each co-owner is said to own a distinct share or a notional proportion of entitlement.
5. Co-ownership in land is governed by the Trusts of Land and Appointment of Trustees Act 1996

6.2 THE JOINT TENANCY

1. In a joint tenancy no tenant owns a specific share.
2. Any transfer of the legal title must be done by all the joint tenants together.
3. There are two main features of the joint tenancy:
   - the right of survivorship (*ius accrescendi*); and
   - the four unities.

6.2.1 The right of survivorship

1. On the death of one of the joint tenants the entire estate passes to the surviving joint tenants.
2. This will continue until there is a sole survivor and the joint tenancy will come to an end.
3. Any attempt to pass a share of a joint tenancy under a will is unenforceable because the joint tenant has no share to leave under his/her will.

4. Under the *commorientes* rule, where two or more persons have died simultaneously it is assumed that the youngest person survived the older (s184 LPA 1925).

5. Under the Law of Property Act s1(6) a legal estate is incapable of existing in divided shares.

6. Since the legal estate automatically vests in the other joint tenants there is no need to formally vest the legal title in the names of the survivors.

6.2.3 The four unities

1. The four unities must be present before a joint tenancy exists.

2. The four unities are: possession, interest, time and title.

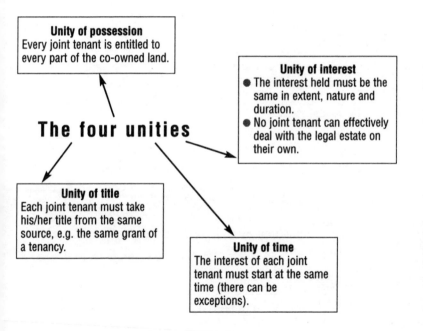

Unity of possession
Every joint tenant is entitled to every part of the co-owned land.

Unity of interest
● The interest held must be the same in extent, nature and duration.
● No joint tenant can effectively deal with the legal estate on their own.

The four unities

Unity of title
Each joint tenant must take his/her title from the same source, e.g. the same grant of a tenancy.

Unity of time
The interest of each joint tenant must start at the same time (there can be exceptions).

6.3 THE TENANCY IN COMMON

1. Under a tenancy in common the co-owners hold specific shares in land, or a proportional share.
2. Although each tenant can claim a share they cannot physically separate the property and claim exclusive possession of their share.
3. Each tenant in common has the right to exercise acts of ownership over the whole property.
4. The doctrine of survivorship does not operate on the death of a tenant in common, and the share can pass under a valid will or intestacy.
5. Only one of the four unities (unity of possession) need be present between tenants in common.

6.3.1 Tenancy in common or joint tenancy?

1. The common law leans in favour of a joint tenancy, but equity leans in favour of a tenancy in common.
2. It was held in *Kinch v Bullard* (1999) that a tenancy in common represents certainty and fairness.
3. Under the LPA 1925 s1(6), s36(2) co-ownership of a legal estate in land must be as a joint tenancy.
4. There can never be severance of the legal estate.
5. There are a number of factors that will indicate whether the equitable estate is held as a joint tenancy or a tenancy in common.
6. Characteristics of an equitable tenancy in common:
    i) Words of severance, e.g. in equal shares or to be divided between.
    ii) One of the four unities absent.
    iii) Contributions of purchase money in unequal shares.
    iv) Two or more commercial partners of business assets are presumed to hold the equitable estate as tenants in common (*Lake v Craddock* (1732)).

v) Lessees of business premises are presumed to hold the premises as tenants in common in equity (*Malayan Credit Ltd v Jack Chia-MPH Ltd* (1986)).

vi) Joint mortgagees who lend money on the security of a mortgage are presumed to hold the equitable estate in the mortgage as tenants in common in equity.

vii) Equity will presume a tenancy in common where there are unequal contributions towards the purchase price between two or more purchasers. The share will be proportional to the size of the contribution.

6.4 METHODS OF SEVERANCE OF THE EQUITABLE ESTATE

6.4.1 Severance by written notice

1. A joint tenant can sever his share by giving to the other joint tenants a written notice of his desire to sever the joint tenancy (s36(2) LPA 1925).

2. This does not need the consent of the other joint tenants to be effective.

3. For severance to be effective it must take effect during the lifetime of the joint tenant.

4. The notice can be in any form, e.g. held in *Re Drapers Conveyance* (1969) that a summons in court proceedings can be sufficient.

5. The notice does not need to be signed or witnessed.

6. It is sufficient to prove that it was actually posted to the other joint tenants, even if it was not actually read by them. In *Kinch v Bullard* (1999), a wife attempted to destroy a notice of severance posted to their home when she heard that her husband had suffered a heart attack. After he died a week later she tried to argue that the notice had not been served. It was held that there had been severance and she was only entitled to a half share.

7. Written severance will not be effective unless it is to take immediate effect, and it must be served on all the joint tenants.

6.4.2 Severance by an act of a joint tenant 'operating upon his share'

1. s36(2) preserves the pre-1925 methods of severance under *Williams v Hensman* (1861).
2. There are three alternatives:
   a) an act operating on a joint tenant's share;
   b) mutual agreement;
   c) mutual conduct.
3. Any act of total or partial alienation of the joint tenant's share will be an act of severance, e.g. sale or mortgage of his/her share or any contract to transfer his/her share.
4. There can be severance where there is an involuntary act of alienation, e.g. bankruptcy.
5. Severance can be brought about when all the joint tenants agree to sever their shares. It must be more than mere discussion, but once there is agreement it need not be in writing or in any special form (*Burgess v Rawnsley* (1975)).
6. Severance can also result from evidence of any course of dealing. 'This course of dealing need not amount to an agreement, expressed or implied for severance' (*Burgess v Rawnsley* (1975), Lord Denning). It is sufficient if there is a course of dealing in which one party makes clear to the other that he desires that their shares should no longer be held jointly but held in common.
7. Negotiations will not be enough to show a course of dealing (*Gore and Snell v Carpenter* (1990)).

6.4.3 Severance by homicide

1. If one joint tenant murders the other joint tenant the tenancy will be severed on the general principle that no one is allowed to profit from their wrongdoing.

2. This will therefore displace the doctrine of survivorship (*Re K dec'd* (1985)).

3. Under the Forfeiture Act 1982 the court has some limited statutory discretion to modify the forfeiture rule, having looked at the surrounding circumstances of the case, e.g. conduct of the offender and of the deceased and other material circumstances.

6.5 CO-OWNERSHIP OF LAND AFTER 1996

6.5.1 Characteristics of a Trust of Land

1. Since 1996, all land in co-ownership is held under a 'trust of land' under the Trusts of Land and Appointments of Trustees Act 1996 (TOLATA).

2. The legal estate can only be held as a joint tenancy. The significance of the legal estate is that the holder of the legal title is entitled to deal in the property.

3. The equitable estate can be held either as a joint tenancy or as a tenancy in common, and the significance of the equitable estate is that it determines the distribution of the beneficial enjoyment.

4. The trustees and beneficiaries of a trust of land can be the same people.

5. The legal estate can only be held by persons who are 18 and over although persons under 18 can hold an equitable estate.

6. The maximum number of trustees of the legal estate is limited to four (s34 LPA 1925). If there is an attempt to transfer the legal estate to more than four then the legal estate will be held by the first four eligible to hold a legal estate named on the conveyance.

7. There is no limit on the number who can hold an equitable estate.

6.5.2 Changes made under the TOLATA 1996

1. Prior to the 1996 Act land held in concurrent ownership was either held in a strict settlement or under a trust for sale.
2. Today, all concurrent ownership of land under a trust whether it is express, implied, resulting or concurrent is held under a trust of land.
3. The 1996 Act prevents the creation of any further strict settlements in land and, today, successive interests in land can only be created under a trust of land.
4. All express trusts for sale created before 1997 continue in existence, but as 'trusts of land', and implied trusts for sale will also automatically become 'trusts of land'.

6.5.3 Powers of the trustees of land

1. The trustees have all the powers of absolute owner. The powers can be expressly excluded.
2. The powers of the trustees must be exercised unanimously or not at all.
3. The trustees have a duty to consult the beneficiaries if of full age, and to give effect to their wishes where possible (s11 TOLATA 1996).
4. The trustees have wide powers to sell, lease and mortgage the legal estate in the trust land.
5. The trustees also have power to purchase a legal estate in land in England and Wales (s6(3) TOLATA 1996).

6.5.4 Rights of the Beneficiaries under a Trust of Land

1. **The right to require express consents** – under s8 there can be a requirement in the trust instrument for consents to be obtained before sale or other disposition.
2. **The right to be consulted:**
   - Under s11 the trustees have a duty to consult the adult beneficiaries so far as is practicable.

- The duty may be restricted by the trust instrument or the court.
- It is only a duty to consult – there is no obligation to comply with their wishes.

3. The right to occupy land (s12 TOLATA):
- beneficiary must be entitled to an interest in possession;
- no right where land has been purchased for investment purposes (*Re Buchanan-Wollaston's Conveyance* (1939));
- trustees can exclude or limit the right to occupy under s13 unless the beneficiary is already in occupation.

4. The right to appoint and remove trustees – Adult beneficiaries under a trust of land who are in agreement can give written directions that one or more of the trustees should retire from the trust, or that a named person should be appointed as trustee (s19 TOLATA).

5. Right to apply for a court order – All beneficiaries have the right to apply to court under the act for an order resolving any disputes in land (s14). They must show that they have an interest in the land.

6.5.5 Overreaching under a trust of land

1. Overreaching allows a purchaser to take free of certain beneficial interests, provided the purchaser complies with the LPA 1925.
2. It is a conveyancing device whereby these beneficial rights are transferred from the land to the purchase money.
3. Certain conditions under the LPA 1925 s2(1) must be satisfied:
   - the conveyance must be made by trustees of land;
   - there must be a conveyance, e.g. a mortgage, lease or sale;
   - the interests must be capable of being overreached, e.g. a beneficial interest under a trust;
   - non-overreachable rights are rights that cannot be exchanged for money, e.g. an easement or a restrictive covenant;
   - the purchaser must comply with s27 LPA and pay over the purchase money to two trustees;

- there are some exceptions, e.g. payment to a trust corporation or a sole personal representative;
- It is also an exception where no payment is made at the time of disposition, e.g. *State Bank of India v Sood* (1997), where the bank made funds available at a future date, but not at the time of charge; held that beneficial rights were overreached.

6.5.6 Effects of Overreaching

1. The purchaser can ignore all interests behind the trust.
2. The beneficial rights can be claimed against the trustees who hold the capital money.
3. The purchaser may be protected if the trustees have failed to get all the requisite consents. Consent from any two named persons will be enough (s10 TOLATA 1996).

6.5.7 Applications to the court under TOLATA 1996

1. An application may be made under s14 by any person who has an interest in the trust property, e.g. the trustees, beneficiaries and a mortgagee.
2. The court may resolve the dispute by 'declaring the nature or extent of any person's interest in the trust land or its proceeds' (s14 TOLATA 1996).
3. s14 is more widely drafted than s30 LPA 1925, which allowed applications to the court and covers a variety of potential applications, e.g. disputes concerning the beneficiaries' right to occupy and any disagreements about sale of the trust land.
4. The court has to have regard to certain criteria laid down in s15 TOLATA 1996 as well as the circumstances and wishes of the beneficiaries.
5. The criteria laid down include:
   a) the intentions of the person or persons who created the trust;

b) the purposes for which the trust land is held;
c) the welfare of any minor who occupies the trust land;
d) the interests of any secured creditor of any beneficiary.

6. Before the 1996 Act the main focus of the law was on the purpose for which the land was bought (*Jones v Challenger* (1961)) and once that purpose had been fulfilled then the court would order sale.

7. Although today the purposes of the trust are one of the criteria considered by the court, the other criteria must be taken into account.

6.5.8 Applications for sale by the creditors

1. Where the beneficiary's trustee in bankruptcy applies for sale, the criteria laid down in TOLATA will not apply.

2. The case is heard in the bankruptcy court, which is directed to make such order as it thinks 'just and reasonable' having regard to the interests of the bankrupt's creditors.

3. Matters that the bankruptcy court will take into account:
- the conduct of the bankrupt's spouse or former spouse so far as contributing to the bankruptcy;
- the needs and financial resources of the spouse or former spouse;
- the needs of any children;
- all the circumstances of the case other than the needs of the bankrupt.

4. In cases decided before the 1996 Act, the trustee in bankruptcy took precedence over the bankrupt's family and an order for sale was usually ordered (*Re Citro (a bankrupt)* (1991)).

5. Even a mortgagee of the family home could obtain an order for sale of that home, in spite of trust beneficiaries holding an overriding interest (*Bank of Baroda v Dhillon* (1998)). In this case the order was made on the basis of the court's jurisdiction under s30 LPA 1925, which predates s15 of TOLATA.

CHAPTER 7

EASEMENTS

Characteristics
Re Ellenborough Park:
- must be dominant/servient tenement;
- must accommodate the dominant tenement;
- dominant/servient tenement must be owned by different persons;
- easement must be capable of forming the subject matter of the grant, e.g. not exclusive use.

The grant of an easement
a) Express grant:
- conveyance;
- statute.
b) Implied grant:
- necessity;
- common intention;
- s62;
- *Wheeldon v Burrows* (quasi-easements).
c) Prescription:
- common law;
- lost modern grant;
- Prescription Act 1832.

EASEMENTS AND PROFITS *A PRENDRE*

Extinguishments of easements
- Extinguished
- Released
- Abandoned

Profits *a prendre*:
- a right to take something from the land;
- can exist without owning land;
- can be created expressly, impliedly (not under the rule in *Wheeldon v Burrows*), by statute and prescription.

Legal and equitable easements
Legal easements:
- must be granted by deed for the equivalent of a legal estate (no deed necessary for implied easements or easements under prescription);
- must be registered in Registered Land even where they are legal.
Equitable easements:
- must be registered to take effect
- no formalities are necessary

7.1 THE CHARACTERISTICS OF EASEMENTS

1. An easement allows someone the right to use the land of another. It can be positive, e.g. a right to use a path over their land, or negative (not requiring any action by the claimant), e.g. a right to light.

2. It is a right that attaches to a piece of land and is not personal to the user.

3. The defining characteristics of an easement are laid down in *Re Ellenborough Park* (1956):

   - there must be a dominant tenement (land to take the benefit) and a servient tenement (land to carry the burden);

   - the easement must accommodate the dominant tenement (this means that it must be a benefit for the land and not a personal benefit for the land owner) (*Hill v Tupper* (1863), *Moody v Steggles* (1879)).

   - the two plots of land should be close to each other;

   - the dominant and servient tenements must be owned by different persons (you cannot have an easement against yourself, but a tenant can have an easement over his landlord's land);

   - the easement must be capable of forming the subject matter of the grant:

     i) there must be a capable grantor and grantee, i.e. people who can grant and receive an easement;

     ii) it must be sufficiently definite, e.g. you cannot have an easement of a good view (*Aldred's Case* (1610)) or an easement of good television reception (*Hunter v Canary Wharf* (1997)).

7.2 OTHER FEATURES OF EASEMENTS

1. The right must not impose any positive burden on the servient owner.

- The duty to fence and to keep the fence in repair is an exception (*Crow v Wood* (1971)).
- A landlord may have to maintain services for a tenant (*Liverpool City Council v Irwin* (1977)).

2. An easement must not amount to exclusive use (*Copeland v Greehalf* (1952)). Storage in a cellar was held to be exclusive use in *Grigsby v Melville* (1972) because it was a right to unlimited storage within a confined or defined space.

3. The right to park can be an easement so long as it is not exclusive use of the property. In *London & Blenheim Estates Ltd v Ladbroke Retail Parks Ltd* (1992), parking in a general area or for a limited period of time could constitute an easement. Parking in a designated space may also be upheld.

4. The courts have been unwilling in the past to extend the list of rights that are capable of existing as easements, although it has been said that easements must adapt to current changes (*Dyce v Lady James Hay* (1852)). However, there was no easement for the reception of television signals in *Hunter v Canary Wharf Ltd* (1997).

7.3 THE GRANT OF AN EASEMENT

An easement can be brought about by:
- express grant,
- implied grant,
- prescription.

7.3.1 Express grant

1. An express grant of an easement is usually through express words incorporated into a transfer of a freehold estate, e.g. in a housing development each purchaser is granted rights covering essential services such as drainage and also rights of way.

2. As the grant is incorporated into a deed of transfer or lease it will take effect at law.

3. Easements can also be expressly granted by estoppel, where the grantee has relied on a promise of rights and acted to his/her detriment (*Crabb v Arun District Council* (1976)).

4. Easements can be expressly granted by statute, e.g. the grant is made in favour of privatised utilities such as the supply of gas or water, or the power to lay sewers.

7.3.2 Implied grant

1. In some circumstances the grant of an easement is implied into the deed of transfer although it is not expressly incorporated.

2. These implied easements will take effect at law because they are implied into the transfer of the legal estate.

3. In registered land they may take effect as overriding interests although circumstances in which they can have been reduced as a result of the LRA 2002.

4. Any easement that is the subject of an implied grant must conform with the characteristics of an easement laid down in *Re Ellenborough Park* (1956).

5. Categories of implied grant:
   a) Easements of necessity
      - Generally easements of necessity imply a right of access.
      - These easements are allowed because without the easement the land would be incapable of use.
      - It will not be available because the alternative route would be inconvenient (*Nickerson v Barraclough* (1981)) only if totally unsuitable for use.
      - Under statute, The Access to Neighbouring Land Act 1992 gives a neighbour the right to seek a court order to gain access to his neighbour's land to carry out essential repairs. This is not automatic and must be applied for through the court.
   b) Easements of common intention
      - Some rights are presumed to be within the intention of the parties and, unless these rights are expressly

excluded, they will be enforceable (*Wong v Beaumont Property Trust Ltd* (1965)). In Wong the premises were intended to be used as a Chinese restaurant. The use of ventilation shafts had to be implied into the grant of the lease otherwise it would contravene public health regulations.

- There must be evidence of intention, but the use need not be necessary for the enjoyment of the property.
- There is an overlap with easements of necessity because easements of common intention will generally only be granted in cases of necessity.

c) The rule under *Wheeldon v Burrows* (1879) provides that where a landowner X divides his land into two plots and sells part of his land over which he/she has enjoyed a benefit, retaining one other part for himself the purchaser Y acquires those benefits over the land retained by X.

- Certain requirements must be satisfied:
  - i) must be continuous and apparent (means the right must be discoverable on careful inspection) and enjoyed over a substantial period of time;
  - ii) must be reasonably necessary for the enjoyment of the property;
  - iii) must be in use at the time of the sale.
- The rule in *Wheeldon v Burrows* converts into easements those rights which are quasi-easements (i.e. those rights which a landowner enjoys over his own land) by implied grant.
- They will take effect as legal easements.
- Under *Re Ellenborough Park* (1956) a landowner cannot enjoy an easement over his own land but quasi-easements can become true easements under this rule.

d) Easements under s62 LPA 1925

- s62 uses general words which, unless expressly excluded, will imply into the conveyance of a legal estate in land a number of rights for the purchaser.

- The section has been interpreted to create new legal easements as well as to transfer those that are already in existence (*International Tea Stores v Hobbs* (1903), where a licence was converted into an easement).
- There must be prior diversity of occupation (*Sovmots Investments Ltd v Secretary of State for the Environment* (1979)).
- s62 operates only on a conveyance of a legal estate.
- The right must come within the definition of an easement, so it must not be a personal user only.
- s62 will not pass a right that was only intended to be temporary (*Wright v Macadam* (1949)).
- s62 will not create an easement if it does not satisfy the requirements in *Re Ellenborough Park* (1956), e.g. it must not be too vague.

7.3.3 Prescription

1. Easements can be acquired from a landowner by use over a long period of time, called prescription.
2. No formalities are necessary to pass the right; it simply requires proof of long use.
3. There are three forms of prescription:
   - common law prescription;
   - the fiction of lost modern grant;
   - under the Prescription Act 1832.
4. Certain rules apply to all types of prescription:
   - the use must be 'as of right', because it is based on the assumption that the right has been passed to the landowner at some time in the past;
   - the use must be *nec vi* (without force), *nec clam* (not exercised in secret), *nec precario* (without permission from the landowner – permission would suggest that the use was not 'of right').
5. Common law prescription presumes that there has been continuous use since 'time immemorial' (set at 1189), but it can be defeated by proof that the use of the right could not be

exercised at any time since 1189. It is rarely successfully argued.

6. The doctrine of 'lost modern grant' supplements common law prescription by allowing an easement to be granted if there is evidence of use over the past 20 years.

● It cannot be used if there was no one who could have made the grant.

● The court accepts that the original grant must have been lost at some date, but this is a legal fiction.

7. The Prescription Act 1832

● Generally regarded as the worst drafted Act of Parliament ever!

● There are two periods under the Act for the acquisition of easements: the short period of 20yrs and the long period of 40yrs.

● Rights acquired under the long period are deemed to be 'absolute and indefeasible' unless permission was granted in writing or by deed.

● Rights acquired under the short period cannot be defeated by evidence that the use commenced after 1189.

● All rights acquired under the Prescription Act must be *nec vi, nec clam* and *nec precario*. They must also satisfy the characteristics of an easement, so a purely personal right could not be acquired prescriptively.

● Under the Prescription Act the period relied on must be the 'next before action'. In *Tehidy Minerals Ltd v Norman* (1971), claims based upon use which ceased in 1941 (because the land had been acquired by the army as part of the war effort) could not be relied on (*Mills v Silver* (1991)).

● Any evidence of interruption will defeat a claim under the Prescription Act.

● Claims under the Prescription Act are only available where there has been litigation.

8. Under s3 of the Prescription Act easements for light can be claimed through proof that there has been actual enjoyment

of access to light for twenty years without interruption

- the right will then be absolute and indefeasible
- proof that it was enjoyed through permission results in the loss of the right.

7.3.4 The reservation of easements

1. The reservation of an easement is the opposite of a grant because the vendor reserves to himself the right to use the land he/she sells to the purchaser.
2. A reservation can be either express or implied.
3. An express reservation will be put into the document of transfer.
4. The reservation is generally construed against the vendor, although some case law suggests this is not always the approach of the courts (*St Edmundsbury and Ipswich Diocesan Board of Finance v Clark (No 2)*(1975)).
5. An implied reservation is only allowed in two cases:
   a) necessity; and
   b) common intention.
6. Cases of implied reservation of easements are very rare.

7.4 LEGAL AND EQUITABLE EASEMENTS

1. Easements may take effect in equity or at law.
2. In order to take effect at law they must satisfy certain rules about the length of time for which they must be created and also the way they are created:
   - s1(2) LPA 1925 legal easements must be granted for a period equivalent to a legal estate in land either a fee simple absolute in possession or a term of years absolute (an easement granted 'for life' can never be a legal easement);
   - s52 LPA 1925 all legal easements must be created by deed. If no deed is used then the grant may take effect in equity;
   - no deed is necessary where rights are acquired by prescription;

- easements that are implied, e.g. by the rule in *Wheeldon v Burrows*, are implied into the deed.

3. An easement will take effect in equity if the requirements for a legal easement are not satisfied.
4. The purchaser may take free of an equitable easement if it has not been registered.
5. Rules concerning the passing of the benefit and burden of an easement are considered in 7.5 below.
6. Under the LRA 2002 equitable easements are no longer overriding. They must be registered as minor interests if they are to be binding.

7.5 THE TRANSFER OF EASEMENTS

1. Easements affect both the dominant (carrying the benefit) and servient (carrying the burden) tenement and can pass to third parties.
2. The transfer of the benefit of an easement will depend on whether it has been created at law or in equity.

7.5.1 The transfer of the benefit and burden of an easement at law

1. The transfer of the benefit of an express legal easement in registered land requires an entry in the Property Register of the land carrying the benefit.
   - Easements acquired by prescription can also be entered in the Property Register once the Land Registrar is satisfied about their validity.
   - Implied easements will still benefit the land but cannot be entered on the Property Register.
2. In unregistered land the benefit of a legal easement automatically passes with any later conveyance of the land.
3. The transfer of the burden in registered land depends on the registration of the right in the Charges Register of the land carrying the burden.

- An easement is a minor interest and so will not be binding until it has been registered.
- Even if it has not been registered a legal easement may still be binding as an overriding interest (*Celsteel Ltd v Alton House Holdings Ltd* (1985) under s70(1)(a) LRA 1925).

4. In unregistered land the burden of a legal easement was automatically binding on the owner of the burdened land.

7.5.2 The transfer of the benefit and burden in equity

1. The transfer of the benefit of an equitable easement either passes under s62 LPA 1925 or expressly.
2. The transfer of the burden will depend on whether the land is registered or unregistered.
3. In registered land the burden of equitable easements must be noted on the Charges Register of the relevant servient title:
   - the decision in *Celsteel Ltd v Alton House Holdings Ltd* (1985) held that an unregistered equitable interest will also take effect as an overriding interest under s70(1)(a) LRA 1925 if the easement was 'openly exercised and enjoyed' at the date of transfer; but after the LRA 2002 this is no longer the case.
4. The LRA 2002 has had considerable impact on the law relating to easements:
   - the benefit of expressly registered easements and profits will have to be registered to be legal under s27(1);
   - the burden of an easement will now rarely be capable of existing as an overriding interest under s70(1)(a);
   - the position differs as to whether it is a first or a subsequent registration;
   - on first registration all legal easements and profits (but not equitable easements) are overriding interests under s1(3);
   - all equitable easements cease to be overriding;
   - on a subsequent registration under s27 LRA all expressly created easements must be registered to be protected;

- only an implied easement can be overriding and only in limited circumstances:
  1. It is registered under the Commons Registration Act 1965.
  2. The acquirer knew of its existence.
  3. The acquirer did not know of it but it would have been obvious on a reasonably careful inspection of the land over which it is exercisable.
  4. Or even if it does not fall within the exceptions it must have been exercised within the period of one year ending with the date of the disposition in question.

5. In unregistered land an equitable easement must be registered as a Class D(iii) land charge against the name of the estate owner who granted the right in question:
   - failure to register an equitable easement in unregistered land makes it void against a purchaser for money or money's worth;
   - the unregistered equitable easement may bind in unregistered land if it is based on estoppel (*E. R. Ives Investment Ltd v High* (1967)).

7.6 THE EXTINGUISHMENT OF EASEMENTS

Extinguished
If the two plots of land come into the same hands, the easement will be extinguished and cannot be revived again even if the land is split in the future.

Released
The easement will cease if the owner of the dominant land gives up the right. This should be in writing for a legal easement, but can be an informal release for an equitable easement.

Easements

Abandoned
Lack of use will not affect the validity of the easement, but it will cease if there is evidence of a clear intention to release the right. It may also be seen as abandoned if there is a change in circumstances making the right redundant.

7.7 PROFITS A PRENDRE

1. A profit *à prendre* entitles the holder to take something from another person's land, e.g. a right to fish or a right to take wood for fuel.

2. Generally, the rules governing profits are similar to the rules concerning easements, but there are one or two features that are different.

3. A profit differs from an easement because it can exist *in gross*, which means it can be personal in nature and the owner does not need to own an estate in land.

   - A profit *in gross* (without ownership of land) can be assigned and conveyed.
   - In registered land a legal profit will rank as an overriding interest.

4. A profit need not be exclusive, so it can be enjoyed in conjunction with others.

5. A profit can be created by express grant, implied grant under s62 LPA 1925 (not the rule in *Wheeldon v Burrows*) and under Statute and Prescription.

6. Profits can exist in law or in equity but for a legal interest they must satisfy the rules, e.g. must be created for the equivalent of a legal estate.

7. The grant must be completed by registration in the same way as for easements.

8. It is possible in rare cases to acquire a profit by implied grant but only under the rules relating to necessity, common intention and s62.

9. The periods for the acquisition of a profit by prescription under the Prescription Act 1832 are 30 years for the short period and 60 years for the long period.

Covenants at law

Running of the benefit:
- 'touch and concerns' the land;
- intention;
- covenantee has legal estate;
- transferee takes legal estate.

Transfers under:
- s136 LPA 1925;
- s56 LPA 1925;
- s78 LPA 1925;
- Contracts (Rights of Third Parties) Act 1999.

Running of the burden – cannot run (*Austerberry v Oldham*).

Avoidance:
- indemnity covenants;
- rule in *Halsall v Brizell*;
- lease;
- conversion from leasehold.

Remedies

- Damages
- Injunction – grounds:
  - i) blatant disregard of rights;
  - ii) extent of injury to rights;
  - iii) oppressive to grant injunction;
  - iv) can it be estimated in money?

RESTRICTIVE COVENANTS

Covenants in equity

Running of the benefit (*Tulk v Moxhay* (1848)):
- must be negative;
- covenantee and covenantor must own estates in land;
- must benefit the land;
- must be intention to bind.

Annexation:
- express;
- implied;
- statutory.

Assignment

Building scheme

Running of the burden:
- purchaser must have notice;
- registered land – notice on Charges Register;
- unregistered land – Class D(ii) against name of covenantor.

Discharge and modification

s84, application to Lands Tribunal on four grounds:
- obsolete;
- no practical benefit;
- agreement;
- no injury suffered.

8.1 THE NATURE OF COVENANTS

1. A covenant is an obligation entered into by deed which restricts the use of land for the benefit of another, e.g. someone's land is not to be used for business purposes.

2. It is an agreement made between the covenantee (who takes the benefit) and the covenantor (who carries the burden).

3. It is governed by the rules of contract as well as the rules of property law:
   - the contract is enforceable between the original parties, but under the privity rule a covenant at common law cannot impose burdens upon a third party.
   - because the covenant is a contract, the original parties continue to be bound even after they have left the property.

4. Equity has intervened to allow the burden of covenants to run in limited circumstances.

8.2 COVENANTS AT LAW

1. Historically, covenants can be traced back to the 14th century (*Priors Case* (1368)).

2. A covenant is enforceable at law even where the covenantor has no estate in law, but the covenantee must have an estate in land that can be benefited.

8.2.1 The passing of the benefit at law

- the covenant must 'touch and concern' the land – the covenant must be for the benefit of the land and not merely for the personal benefit of the covenantee (*P & A Swift Investments v Combined English Stores Group Plc* (1989));
- there must have been an intention that the benefit should run with the estate owned by the covenantee at the date of the covenant (*Smith and Snipes Hall Farm*

Ltd v River Douglas Catchment Board (1939), presumed under s78 LPA 1925);

- the covenantee must have a legal interest in the dominant land – no benefit can pass where the original covenantee has an equitable interest in the land;
- the transferee of the dominant land must also take a legal estate in that land – any legal estate in land will give the transferee the right to enforce the covenant.

8.2.2 Transferring the benefit of covenants at law

1. s136 LPA 1925 allows for the express assignment of a covenant as a chose in action, but it must be in writing. This is rare as there are other ways of assigning the benefit that are more convenient.
2. s56 LPA 1925 allows the benefit to pass to others who, though not mentioned expressly in the conveyance, are expressed to be those for whose benefit the covenant was made, e.g. plots 1–7 are sold and a clause is added in plot 2 to pass the benefit of a covenant to the owner of plot 2, but is worded to cover plots 3–7 as well.
3. s56 does not allow a benefit to be passed to future purchasers.
4. s78 LPA 1925 has been interpreted to be effective to pass the benefit of a covenant to a third party:
   - it will only cover covenants that 'touch and concern' the covenantee's land;
   - it only relates to covenants entered into after 1925;
   - it is only for the benefit of owners for the time being.
5. The Contracts (Rights of Third Parties) Act 1999 has made extensions to the rights of any third party in covenants entered into after May 2000:
   - a person who is not a party to the contract can now enforce the contract on his own behalf if either it expressly confers a benefit on him, or the term purports to confer a benefit on him but does not refer to him by name;

- it cannot be enforced if, on the proper construction of the contract, it appears that the parties did not intend the benefit to be enforceable;
- the third party must either be named or be referred to generically, e.g. to X (owner of No. 2) and her successors, and the owners of No. 3 and No. 4 (the neighbouring properties). As there is no contrary intention shown then the contract appears to confer a benefit on the owners of Nos 3 and 4.

8.2.3 Transmission of the burden at law

1. The common law has always maintained a clear rule that the burden of a covenant cannot run with the freehold land of the covenantor (*Austerberry v Oldham Corp* (1885)).
2. The rule has been subject to criticism over the years, but was confirmed in *Rhone v Stephens* (1994): Nourse LJ – 'the rule is hard to justify' (Court of Appeal), but Lord Templeman held it to be 'inappropriate for the courts to overrule the Austerberry case, which has provided the basis for transactions relating to the rights and liabilities of landowners for over 100 years...' (House of Lords).

8.2.4 Avoiding the rule in Austerberry

1. The doctrine of mutual benefit and burden – if a purchaser takes certain benefits under the conveyance, then the purchaser cannot avoid the burdens of an associated covenant (the rule in *Halsall v Brizell* (1957), *Tito v Waddell* (No. 2)(1977)).
2. Chain of indemnity covenants – the covenantor remains liable and can be sued even after sale if the original covenantor and each successive owner of the burdened land obtains an appropriately worded indemnity covenant from his purchaser. The continuing liability of the original covenantor can be indemnified by the party actually in breach of the covenant.

3. Lease – the burden of both positive and negative covenants can run with leasehold land.
4. Conversion of leaseholds into freeholds – rarely used and seen as artificial, but all the covenants under the lease will be enforceable by the covenantee.

8.3. COVENANTS IN EQUITY

8.3.1 The decision in *Tulk v Moxhay* (1848)

1. The claimant sold a vacant piece of land in Leicester Square with notice of a covenant restricting the use of the land (the covenantor agreed to maintain the square as a garden). The purchaser tried to build on the property.
2. It was held that the owners of the neighbouring benefited land had a right in equity to enforce the covenant against the purchaser because he knew of the covenant when he bought the land.

8.3.2 The rules derived from *Tulk v Moxhay*

1. The covenant must be negative.
   - A restrictive covenant is a covenant that does not require expenditure of money.
   - Some covenants appear to be negative but are positive, e.g. not to let the property fall into disrepair is a positive covenant. Maintenance of the property would require expenditure of money.
2. At the date of the covenant, the covenantee must own the land to be benefited by the covenant, and the covenantor must own an estate to carry the burden (*LCC v Allen* (1914)).
3. At law, a covenant can pass even where the covenantor has no estate in land, but the right would not pass in equity.
4. The covenant must benefit or accommodate the dominant tenement. This means that it must affect the value of the land and must not be a personal benefit to the owner of the land.

5. The parties must have intended the burden to bind the successors. It is generally presumed that the burden was intended to run with the land of the covenantor (s79(1) LPA 1925).

8.3.3 The passing of the benefit of a covenant in equity

1. The covenant must pass under one of the ways allowed by equity.
2. This was once fraught with legal technicalities, but today is relatively straightforward.
3. There are three ways of passing the benefit in equity:
- annexation;
- assignment;
- a building scheme.

8.3.4 Annexation

1. This is a process where the benefit of a restrictive covenant is metaphorically 'nailed' or attached to a clearly defined area of land belonging to the covenantee, so the benefit will pass with the land at all subsequent sales.
2. Express annexation occurs where there is an express intention in the words of the covenant that the benefit should pass (*Re Ballard's Conveyance* (1937)). Once it has been expressly annexed, then on division of the land the benefit of the covenant will still pass.
3. Implied annexation is rare but will occur when the intention to attach the benefit is clearly implicit in the circumstances of the case (*Newton Abbot Co-operative Society Ltd v Williamson & Treadgold Ltd* (1952)).
4. Statutory annexation has made express and implied annexation far less important because of the relative ease with which a covenant can be said to be annexed under statute. In *Federated Homes Ltd v Mill Lodge Properties Ltd* (1980), the

restrictive covenant was deemed to pass under s78 LPA 1925 once it was shown that the covenant 'touched and concerned' the land.

5. Under s78 covenants are automatically annexed, making the express assignment and annexation redundant.

6. Annexation will not be automatic where the parties include a contrary intention in the conveyance, and expressly restrict the passing of the benefit to successors in title (*Roake v Chadha* (1984)).

7. Pre-1926 covenants will also not pass automatically with the land under s78 (*J Sainsbury Plc v Enfield LBC* (1989)).

8.3.5 Assignment

1. Assignment differs from annexation because the covenant is annexed to the person rather than the land.

2. It also differs from annexation because it is made on subsequent transfers of the land, perhaps some years after the making of the covenant, whereas annexation takes place when the covenant is first made.

3. There should be a fresh assignment at each subsequent sale and there should be an unbroken chain of assignments.

4. The covenant must be taken for the protection or benefit of land owned by the covenantee at the date of the covenant.

5. The assignment must be at the same time as the transfer of the dominant land.

8.3.6 Scheme of development

1. A scheme of development overcomes the problems of a property developer leaving a development, having entered into a number of covenants with each purchaser but no longer retaining servient land against which actions can be brought for breach of covenant.

2. Under a scheme of development, restrictive covenants are enforceable against each current owner of land:

- it does not matter whether the covenant was made by the original covenantee or a successor in title;
- in order to take effect under the building scheme the covenants must be registered either at the Land Registry or the Land Charges Registry;
- under the LRA 2002 new covenants passing under a scheme of development will only be registered at the Land Registry.

3. Preconditions for a scheme of development were once very technical and difficult to satisfy (*Elliston v Reacher* (1908)).
4. Today the conditions are much easier to satisfy:
   - there must be an identifiable scheme. This means there must be a defined area of land over which reciprocal obligations were intended to be enforceable, but the area does not have to be laid out in lots before a scheme can be found (*Baxter v Four Oaks Properties Ltd* (1965));
   - it must be shown that all the purchasers bought property with the intention to be bound by the covenants even if they did not buy from a common vendor (*Re Dolphin's Conveyance* (1970)).

8.4 THE PASSING OF THE BURDEN IN EQUITY

1. The burden will pass in equity if the purchaser has notice of the covenant.
   - In *Tulk v Moxhay* this meant actual notice because it was decided before the property legislation of 1925.
   - A purchaser for value of the legal estate without notice of the covenant was not bound by the covenant.
2. After 1925 it depends on whether the covenant has been registered.
   - In registered land a 'notice' should be entered in the Charges Register of the covenantor's title (LRA 1925 s20).

- In unregistered land the covenant should be registered against the name of the covenantor as a Class D(ii) land charge (LCA 1972 s2(5)).

3. Failure to register will render the covenant unenforceable even where the purchaser has actual notice.

8.5 DISCHARGE AND MODIFICATION OF RESTRICTIVE COVENANTS

1. Under s84 LPA 1925 an application to discharge or modify a restrictive covenant may be made to the Lands Tribunal.

2. The party applying must establish one of four grounds:
   - the restrictive covenant should be deemed 'obsolete because of the changes in character in the neighbourhood' or other relevant circumstances, e.g. if a former residential area now has mixed use then a covenant against business use may now be obsolete (s84(1)(aa));
   - the covenant impedes a reasonable user and does not provide 'any practical benefit of substantial value or advantage to any person or is contrary to the public interest' (s84(1)(a));
   - those entitled to the benefit of the covenant have agreed to its discharge or modification (s84 (1)(b));
   - the discharge or modification will not injure the persons entitled to the benefit of the covenant (s84 (1)(c)).

3. If the tribunal agrees to discharge or modify the covenant on any grounds it may order compensation to be paid to the owners of the benefited land.

4. The fact that planning permission has already been granted for a development does not mean that the Lands Tribunal will automatically discharge a covenant.

5. Refusal to discharge a covenant by the Lands Tribunal may be one way that a development may be curtailed by concerned neighbours.

6. A restrictive covenant will no longer be enforceable where the land comes into single ownership.

8.6 REMEDIES FOR BREACH OF A RESTRICTIVE COVENANT

1. If a claimant proves that a covenant has been broken then damages will be available.
2. In some cases an equitable remedy e.g. an injunction, will be sought and the court will make the decision on the following criteria:
   * Has there been a blatant disregard for the claimant's rights?
   * Is the injury to the claimant's legal rights small?
   * Can the damage can be estimated in money and can it be adequately compensated by a small money payment?
   * Will it be oppressive to the defendant to grant an injunction? In *Gafford v Graham* (1998) an injunction was sought, but the injunction was refused and £25,000 in damages was awarded although it was argued that to refuse an injunction was to 'licence future wrongs'.
3. An injunction will not automatically be awarded where there is a breach of covenant (*Jaggard v Sawyer* (1995)).
4. Courts have been prepared to grant a mandatory injunction to demolish a building (*Wakeham v Wood* (1982)). However this is rare.

8.7 THE REFORM OF COVENANTS

1. As early as 1965 the Law Commission noted that most positive covenants were wholly unenforceable and the law should be reformed (*Report of the Committee on Positive Covenants Affecting Land 1965*).
2. In 1984 proposals were made for a new 'land obligation' allowing positive and negative obligations to be imposed on a piece of land.
   * The rights would be either 'neighbour obligations' (for two neighbours) or 'development obligations' (for multi-occupation).

- The rights would need registration and, once registered, would be binding but would be enforceable only between the current owners of the respective tenements.

3. It has also been suggested that covenants should be automatically extinguished after a statutorily fixed period has expired. The Law Commission suggested 80 years in 1991 (*Transfer of Land: Obsolete Restrictive Covenants*). There would be a right to appeal by the owner of the right.

4. A further suggestion has been for a 'commonhold scheme' to allow rights to attach to land within the scheme. This would allow both positive and negative obligations to be enforceable.

5. There are no immediate plans for any of these reforms to come into law.

Creation of legal mortgage
Registered land:
● charge by way of legal mortgage;
Unregistered land:
● deed;
● deposit of title deeds;
● demise of a term of years.
Now triggers registration of title.

Creation of equitable mortgage
a) Equitable interest in land.
b) Equitable charge.
c) Incomplete legal mortgage.
d) Deposit of documents of title.
e) Charging order.
f) Unpaid vendor's or purchasers lien.

MORTGAGES

Protection for mortgagor
a) Protecting right to redeem.
b) Striking down oppressive interest rates.
c) Preventing extortionate credit agreements.
d) Preventing unfair collateral advantages.
e) The court may set aside any transaction which has been induced by undue influence.

Priority
Depends on:
● whether mortgage is legal or equitable;
● whether the title is registered or unregistered.

Rights of the mortgagee
a) Possession.
b) Action on covenant to repay.
c) Appointment of a receiver.
d) Power to sell.
e) Foreclosure.

9.1 DEFINITION OF MORTGAGES

1. A mortgage of land is the conveyance or transfer of land made to secure the future repayment of a loan or the discharge of some other obligation.
2. The land is transferred to the lender but subject to the provision for redemption, which is a provision that once the loan has been repaid the transfer becomes void or the land is transferred back to the borrower.
3. The borrower (the mortgagor) grants the mortgage to the lender (the mortgagee).

9.2 THE DEVELOPMENT OF MORTGAGES AT COMMON LAW AND IN EQUITY

9.2.1 The common law

1. Before 1926 the owner of land who took out a mortgage actually conveyed the land to the lender with a stipulation that, on a certain date, the mortgagee would reconvey the property back to the mortgagor.
2. The repayment had to be on the date agreed and there was no scope for varying the date.
3. Failure to repay on the agreed date meant loss of the property even if the value of the property was far more than the outstanding amount on the loan.

9.2.2 Equity

1. Equity modified the effects of the common law in the 17th century and allowed the repayment to be made after the redemption date, called the 'equitable right to redeem'.
2. The mortgagor also remained the owner of the property even during the currency of the loan, but subject to the loan.

3. If the mortgagee went into possession of the property then he had to account for any profit made.

9.3 THE CREATION OF MORTGAGES

9.3.1 Legal mortgages and charges

1. Legal mortgages can only be created where the borrower has a legal interest (fee simple or term of years) in the property.

2. In registered land a legal mortgage is created by a registered charge which can take two different forms.

  a) The most usual form is a charge by way of legal mortgage:
- this is effective at law once it has been registered by the chargee entering as the proprietor of the charge in the Charges Register;
- if it is not registered then it will only be effective in equity and will take effect as a minor interest requiring protection by notice or caution.

  b) It is also possible to create a mortgage by 'charge by way of demise of a term of years', which means that the mortgagee gets a leasehold interest of 3000 years in the property. This highly artificial means of creating a mortgage is rarely used today. This is now abolished in the LRA 2002 for registered land.

3. In unregistered land, legal mortgages can be created either by deed or by demise, as in registered land.

4. A first legal mortgage of an unregistered freehold or leasehold land executed after 1 April 1998 will trigger a requirement of first registration at HM Registry.
- If there is no application for first registration of the mortgagor's estate within two months, then the mortgage will lapse as a disposition of a legal charge.
- The mortgagor will still have a legal estate but it will merely be a contract to create a legal charge and will take effect in equity only.

5. Historically, mortgages in unregistered land were made by deposit of title deeds, as this was an effective safeguard against

attempts to deal in the estate without notifying the first
mortgagee.

- These mortgages, if made after 1 April 1998, will trigger
  first registration of title
- Mortgages made prior to this date should have been
  registered at the Land Charges Registry as a Class C(i)
  land charge if they wished to have priority over other
  charges.
- It is the only legal interest in land (called a puisne
  mortgage) that could be registered at the Land Charges
  Registry.
- Today the creation of a mortgage will always act as a
  trigger for compulsory registration of the property.

9.3.2 The creation of equitable mortgages

1. There are many different forms of equitable mortgage.
   - A mortgage of a borrower's equitable interest in land –
     this must be equitable because the borrower only has an
     equitable estate, e.g. a beneficial interest under a trust of
     land.
   - An informal or incomplete mortgage of a legal estate in
     land – e.g. a defect in the creation of a legal mortgage or
     failure to register the charge at the Registry.
   - An equitable charge – land charged with an obligation,
     such as the repayment of a debt, but unlike a mortgage no
     property passes to the chargee, only the right to sue for
     the debt.
   - A mortgage by deposit of documents of title, coupled with
     a written and signed contract of loan – prior to the
     LP(MP) Act 1989 a mortgage could be created by
     depositing title deeds without the need for written
     documents (*Russel v Russel* (1783)). Today there must be a
     written contract.
   - A charging order under the Charging Orders Act 1979 –
     an order for a charge to be to be placed on property

granted by the County or High Court giving the chargee the right to seek an order for sale.

- An unpaid vendor's lien over the subject matter of sale – the vendor retains a lien over the property until the purchase price is paid. It does not transfer rights in the property but a right to seek judgement at court.
- A purchaser's lien to secure title – arises once the deposit is paid.

9.4 PROTECTION FOR THE MORTGAGOR

1. There are four main ways that equity has attempted to protect the mortgagor:
   - protecting the equitable right to redeem;
   - striking down oppressive interest rates;
   - preventing extortionate credit bargains;
   - preventing unfair collateral advantages.

9.4.1 Protecting the equitable right to redeem

1. The mortgagor has the right to redeem the mortgage on the contractual date for redemption.
2. Equity gave the mortgagor the right to redeem after the date for redemption had passed and the legal right to redeem was lost.
3. The courts have struck down any attempt to 'fetter the equity of redemption' (*Biggs v Hoddinott* (1898)).
4. Attempts to postpone the contractual date for redemption may be struck down where it results in reduction of value of the asset, e.g. a leasehold property (*Fairclough v Swan Brewery Co Ltd* (1912)).

9.4.2 Oppressive interest rates

1. Mortgagees can reserve to themselves the right to vary the interest at any time.

2. Control by the courts of oppressive interest rates depends largely on their inherent jurisdiction to declare any mortgage term 'void' if it is 'oppressive' or 'unconscionable'.
3. When the court reviews interest rates, they will only vary them if it sees the mortgagor is in a weaker bargaining position than the mortgagee (*Cityland and Property (Holdings) Ltd v Dabrah* (1968)).
4. A borrower of 'intelligence' and a 'man of business' could not successfully challenge an interest rate of 50% (*Carringtons Ltd v Smith* (1906)).

9.4.3 Extortionate credit agreements

1. Protection for mortgagors against unconscionable credit agreements is provided by the Consumer Credit Act 1974.
2. This act gives the courts the power to reopen 'extortionate' credit bargains.
3. Generally, a mortgage of land is not a 'consumer credit agreement' unless it comes within the definition of 'extortionate'.
4. Once the court declares the credit agreement to be extortionate it is reopened and, unless the creditor proves that it was not extortionate, the court will set aside any part or the whole of the agreement.
5. The court determines the issue in the light of prevailing interest rates at the time and the personal conditions of the borrower, e.g. is he/she elderly, in good health, under financial pressure, etc.?

9.4.4 Unfair collateral advantages

1. Equity has always prevented any attempt to put a 'clog or fetter' on the effective exercise of the mortgagor's equity of redemption.

2. The modern view is that these terms will only be unlawful if they are:
   - unfair and unconscionable; or
   - in the nature of a penalty clogging the equity of redemption; or
   - inconsistent with, or repugnant to the contractual and equitable right to redeem.
3. A collateral advantage that is not part of the mortgage at all will be outside the principle that it 'clogs the equity of redemption'. If the collateral advantage is a wholly independent transaction then it is enforceable even beyond the redemption of the mortgage, so long as it is not shown to be unconscionable.

9.5 UNDUE INFLUENCE IN A MORTGAGE TRANSACTION

1. The court may set aside any transaction that has been induced by undue influence (*Barclay's Bank v O'Brien* (1994)).
2. Undue influence can be either:
   - actual undue influence;
   - presumed undue influence.

9.5.1 Actual undue influence

1. The complainant must prove that undue influence was exerted over him to enter into the particular transaction.
2. In these cases there is no need to show that the transaction was to the victim's manifest disadvantage.

9.5.2 Presumed undue influence

1. In these cases the complainant only has to show that there was a relationship of trust and confidence between the wrongdoer and the complainant.
2. The relationship was of such a nature that it is fair to presume that the wrongdoer abused that relationship to persuade the complainant to enter into the transaction.

3. The burden of proof shifts to the wrongdoer to show that there was no undue influence, e.g. by showing that the complainant received independent advice.

4. The relationship may take one of two forms:

   a) automatic presumption of undue influence as a matter of law in certain kinds of relationship, e.g. solicitor and client, doctor and patient;

   b) presumption based on the *de facto* existence of a relationship under which the complainant generally placed 'trust and confidence in the wrongdoer' (*Barclays Bank plc v O'Brien* (1994)):

   - the transaction can be set aside on the mere proof that the complainant placed trust and confidence in the wrongdoer;

   - it is not necessary to show that there is actual undue influence or that the wrongdoer abused it in relation to the transaction;

   - examples of relationships which give rise to the presumption in (b) would be son and elderly parents, cohabiting partners (either homosexual or heterosexual);

   - in these cases it must generally be shown that the transaction was of manifest disadvantage to the complainant (*Nat West Bank plc v Morgan* (1985)).

   c) since *Royal Bank of Scotland v Etridge* (2001) the mortgagee will be put on inquiry in every case where the relationship between the borrower and their surety is non-commercial.

5. The borrower may claim to have the transaction set aside if there is evidence that the lender had actual or constructive notice of the undue influence:

   - constructive notice will be proved if, on its face, the transaction was not to the financial advantage of the borrower; or

   - there is a substantial risk that the primary debtor (e.g. the husband) may have committed a legal wrong which would then entitle the surety to set aside the transaction.

6. The lender can resist the setting aside of the transaction if he can prove either that the complainant attended a private interview explaining the risks of the situation or was given some independent legal advice. The mortgagee does not have to attend a personal interview with the surety.

- the mortgagee can rely on confirmation from a solicitor acting for the surety that he has given advice;
- the mortgagee will not be liable for negligent advice given by the solicitor unless he is aware that the solicitor has given proper advice or he knows that the solicitor is not fully aware of all the facts.

9.6 RIGHTS OF THE MORTGAGEE

9.6.1 The right to take possession

1. The mortgagee has a right to take immediate possession of the mortgaged property. 'The mortgagee can go into possession before the ink is dry on the paper' (Harman J in *Four-Maids Ltd v Dudley Marshall (Properties) Ltd* (1957)). This will operate where the mortgagor defaults in repayment.
2. Institutional lenders such as Building Societies do not want possession for themselves but want to sell the property.
3. A mortgagee who goes into possession will be subject to the stringent control of equity.
4. Most mortgage agreements only allow the right to take possession where there has been default by the mortgagor.
5. The payment of the sum owed must be payable by instalments and not repaid in full when the mortgagee demands.
6. The court has an inherent power to postpone possession proceedings to give the mortgagor a limited opportunity to find the means to pay the debt (28 days).
7. There are also statutory powers to stay proceedings under s36 Administration of Justice Act 1970, which protects homeowners from repossession for such time as the court thinks is reasonable.

8. The court will only stay proceedings if there is a realistic chance of the mortgagor repaying the sum outstanding although this may not be the entire sum (*Cheltenham & Gloucester Building Society v Norgan* (1996), s8 Administration of Justice Act 1973).

9.6.2 Other remedies open to the mortgagee

1. Action on the mortgagor's covenant to repay – this arises under contract. Interest will be statute-barred after six years (LA 1980 s20).

2. Appointment of a receiver
   - The receiver will handle the income of the mortgaged property, but is under a less strict duty than a mortgagor in possession.
   - The power to appoint receivers will be in the mortgage deed.
   - The date for redemption must have passed.
   - Must be in writing.
   - s109 LPA governs the making of payments from the income by the receiver.

3. Exercise of the power to sell
   - ss101–104 expressly conferred in a mortgage deed.
   - The legal date for redemption must have passed or some instalment of the mortgage money must have become due.
   - Three conditions to be satisfied:
     a) notice served by the mortgagees;
     b) interest due under the mortgage is two months in arrears;
     c) the mortgagors have breached some term under the mortgage deed.
   - s105 deals with the proceeds of sale which must be paid in order of priority of the mortgages. Any outstanding amount can be claimed personally. The mortgagee is

under a duty to obtain a proper price, e.g. *Raja v Lloyds TSB Bank plc* (2001) Lloyds Rep Bank 113.

- A receiver may be appointed as they will be responsible for the sale.

4. Foreclosure – this is the most draconian remedy open to the mortgagee. It leaves the entire value of the mortgaged property in the hands of the mortgagee. Must make an application to the court. Extremely rare today. It allows the mortgagee to retain any increase in value of the property.

9.7 PRIORITY OF MORTGAGES

1. If there is more than one mortgage in the property and the borrower defaults, prompting one of the lenders to sell the property, the priority of the other lenders is governed by two factors:

- are the mortgages legal or equitable; and
- is the title to the property registered or unregistered?

9.7.1 Unregistered land

1. A legal mortgage with title deeds will bind all subsequent mortgages.
2. A legal mortgage will take priority over an earlier equitable mortgage if he/she had no notice of it.
3. Where both mortgages are equitable then the first in time will generally prevail.
4. If the first equitable mortgage is not protected by title deeds then it must be registered and, if it is not properly registered, it will lose priority over a later mortgage.
5. Mortgages of an equitable estate are governed by the rule in *Dearle v Hall* (1823), i.e. the order in which notice of the mortgages is received by the trustees of the land.

9.7.2 Registered land

1. There is only one way of mortgaging a legal estate and that is by way of registered charge.
2. Registered charges will rank according to the order in which they are entered on the register and not according to the time when they were created.
3. An equitable mortgage must be registered as a minor interest.
4. Failure to protect the rights results in them losing priority over subsequent rights even where there is actual or constructive notice of them. If properly registered, then the charge will take priority over any legal charge later taken over the property
5. Where there are two equitable mortgages, priority is decided not by entry on the register but by the date of creation.
6. The rule in *Dearle v Hall* (1823) will also apply where there is a mortgage of an equitable estate with registered title.

9.7.3 Example

Greenacre
X holds legal charge dated Jan 5 but registered Jan 26.
Y holds legal charge dated Jan 15 but registered Jan 20.

Priority: 1 – Y
       2 – X

Whiteacre
X holds an equitable charge dated Jan 15 which is unregistered.
Y holds a legal charge dated Jan 25 and it is registered Jan 25.
Z holds an equitable charge dated Jan 10 and it is registered Jan 10.
A holds a legal charge dated Jan 30 and it is registered Jan 30.

Priority: 1 – Z
       2 – Y
       3 – A
       4 – X

CHAPTER 10

LEASES

Characteristics of a lease:
- exclusive possession;
- for a term;
- at a rent.

Creation of a lease must be in writing and by deed unless less than three years.

Leases for more than seven years are registrable legal estates in land.

Distinction between a lease and licence
- Lease gives a proprietary estate.
- Licence gives a personal right to occupy.
- Significance lies in:
  i) statutory protection;
  ii) right to assign;
  iii) right to enforce covenants;
  iv) right to buy.

LEASES

Termination of leases:
a) notice to quit;
b) forfeiture;
c) surrender;
d) disclaimer;
e) expiry;
f) frustration;
g) merger;
h) repudiation;
i) use of a 'break clause'.

Regulation of leases
Express covenants.
Implied covenants:
- quiet enjoyment;
- derogation from the grant.

Common law implied covenants for repair.
Statutory obligations:
- to keep in good repair;
- ss8–10 LTA 1985;
- ss11–16 LTA 1985;
- Defective Premises Act 1972.

Enforcement
a) Before 1995 covenants enforceable against T even after assignment.
b) After 1995 covenants no longer enforceable after assignment. Cannot be varied by parties. No release if excluded assignment or authorised guarantee agreement.
c) After 1995 still liability for breaches occurring before assignment.

Remedies for breach of covenant
Landlord:
- forfeiture;
- injunction/specific performance;
- sue for damages.

Tenant:
- damages;
- specific performance;
- self-help and set-off.

10.1 THE CHARACTERISTICS OF A LEASE

1. Under the LPA 1925 the term of years absolute is a legal estate in land and is also a proprietary estate in land.
2. A lease or tenancy has been very difficult to define and there is no adequate statutory definition.
3. Case law (*Street v Mountford* (1985); *Prudential Assurance Co Ltd v London Residuary Body* (1992)) suggests that a lease has three main identifying features:
   - exclusive possession of land;
   - a determinate period;
   - rent or other consideration, although this has been doubted in recent decisions.

10.1.1 Exclusive possession

1. This means that the tenant has control over who enters the premises and can exclude everyone, including the landlord.
2. A tenant can still have exclusive possession even if he can be required to vacate the premises for a period each day (*Aslan v Murphy* (1990)).
3. Sole occupancy of land is not the same as exclusive possession (*Westminster City Council v Clarke* (1992)). The court will look at the nature of the accommodation when deciding if there is a lease. In *Clarke* there was no exclusive possession of a room in a council hostel for single men because residents could be required to change rooms at will.
4. The retention of a key by the landlord does not necessarily mean that there is no exclusive possession if it is solely for access to carry out repairs or for emergencies (*Aslan v Murphy* (1990)).
5. A key retained so the landlord can use the premises for his own purposes will negate exclusive possession.
6. A lodger does not enjoy exclusive possession (*A-G Securities v Vaughan* (1990)). Lodgings usually suggest that services are

provided, e.g. the collection of rubbish or the cleaning of windows.

7. There will not be exclusive possession if premises are provided by the employer for the better performance of a job.

8. Where purchasers are let into possession prior to completion of a purchase of premises there is no exclusive possession.

9. There may be exclusive possession even where the landlord does not have an estate to support a lease. (In *Bruton v London & Quadrant Housing Trust* (1999), the landlord had a mere licence but the landlord still had the right to create a lease in favour of the claimant.)

10.1.2 A determinate period

1. The maximum duration of the lease must be fixed from the start of the term.

2. Property let for uncertain periods, e.g. for the duration of the war (*Lace v Chandler* (1944)) will not constitute a lease.

3. A clause allowing the lease to be determined before the expiry of the full term granted will not cause it to fail as a lease.

4. Leases for lives and leases until marriage are statutorily converted into a 90 year term determinable on the death or marriage of the original lessee (LPA 1925 s146).

5. A perpetually renewable lease is converted automatically into a term of 2000 years, determinable only by the lessee.

6. A periodic tenancy can exist as a tenancy even though there is no fixed term of maximum duration (*Prudential Assurance Co Ltd v London Residuary Body* (1992)).

7. The reason a periodic tenancy can exist as a tenancy is because it is regarded as running for the period of the term of tenancy and then it is renewed for a further term (*Hammersmith and Fulham LBC v Monk* (1992)).

8. An example of a periodic tenancy: X grants Y a weekly tenancy – the law regards the period of the lease as one week, but renewable with the agreement of the parties at the end of every week.

10.1.3 The obligation to pay rent

1. Historically, this was an essential feature of a lease and it would be implied where it was not expressly included.
2. In *Street v Mountford* (1985) it was held to be one of the hallmarks of a tenancy.
3. This has later been disputed in *Ashburn Anstalt v Arnold* (1989) and also in *Westminster C.C. v Clarke* (1992). The most recent decision on the issue (*Bruton v London & Quadrant Housing Trust* (2000)) upholds the principle that rent is not necessary for the creation of a tenancy, although in practice rent is usually payable.
4. Rent need not be adequate and could be in a form other than money, e.g. in kind.
5. Rent must be certain on the date for payment.
6. A rent review clause can be included which varies the amount to be paid, but if rent can be varied arbitrarily it suggests that a licence exists (*Dresden Estates v Collinson* (1988)).

10.2 THE DISTINCTION BETWEEN A LEASE AND A LICENCE

1. The main differences between a lease and a licence:
   - **a lease** confers a proprietary estate, which gives the tenant an exclusive right of possession;
   - **a licence** does not confer a proprietary estate, but merely gives a personal permission to occupy.
2. The main similarities between the two are that they both confer a right to exclusive occupation of land in exchange for consideration.
3. The distinction between the two has become less marked in recent years.

10.2.1 The significance of the lease/licence distinction in law

1. A tenant can assign his interest in land and the lease is enforceable against the original lessor.
2. If the lessor transfers his interest in land, then the lease is capable of binding the transferee. A lease over seven years will be registrable but a lease under seven years will be overriding.
3. A licensee cannot claim statutory protection under the landlord and tenant legislation, e.g. the Rent Act 1977, The Landlord and Tenant Act 1954 (business tenants only), although they have some protection under the Housing Act 1985.
4. Residential tenants under long leases may have the right to purchase the freehold.
5. Tenants have the right to enforce repairing covenants in the lease unavailable to licensees (Landlord and Tenant Act 1985).
6. The Protection from Eviction Act 1977 will protect licensees as well as lessees.

10.2.2 The parties' intentions

1. The tenancy is an agreement between the two parties and is subject to the usual requirements of a valid contract.
2. The courts look at the true intent of the parties.
3. They ignore the terms used by the parties such as a 'licence' or a 'tenancy' (*Street v Mountford* (1985)). This was a deciding issue in *Somma v Hazelhurst* (1978). In *Bruton v London & Quadrant Housing Trust* (2000) Lord Hoffman said 'the fact the parties use language more appropriate to a different kind of agreement, such as a licence, is irrelevant if upon its true construction it has the identifying characteristics of a lease...'.
4. The courts seek to draw a distinction between those agreements that are a mere sham and those that are a genuine transaction.

10.3 THE CREATION OF A LEASE

10.3.1 Formalities in the creation

1. Both parties must be legally competent, e.g. a minor cannot hold a legal estate in land.
2. If a minor takes a lease then that will take effect as an equitable estate in land.
3. The subject matter of the lease must be certain.
4. The formalities for the transfer of a legal estate in land must be complied with: 'no interest in land can be created or disposed of except by writing signed by the person creating or conveying the same...' (LPA 1925 s53(1)(a)). The conveyance must also be created by deed (s52(1) LPA 1925).
5. A lease for less than three years does not require writing if it is 'at the best rent which can be reasonably obtained without taking a fine' and possession is immediate (a fine means a premium or lump sum of money).
6. Failure to comply with the necessary formalities results in the lease taking effect in equity only.
7. A periodic tenancy can be created orally on the basis that the period is less than three years.
8. An assignment of a term of years (even if the estate was created orally) can only be done in writing (*Crago v Julian* (1992)).

10.3.2 Registration of the leasehold estate

1. Where a leasehold estate is for a period in excess of seven years LRA (2002) then the interest must be registered at the Land Registry, irrespective of whether the freehold title is registered or unregistered before it can gain legal status.
2. If the term is not registered within two months of the grant it will lose its legal status and will take effect in equity only.
3. Normally the title will be registered with absolute leasehold title

4. If this cannot be given then a good leasehold title will be registered, which means that it will be subject to any 'estate, right or interest affecting or in derogation of the title of the lessor to grant the lease' (LRA 1925 s10).

5. A lease for less than seven years cannot be registered, nor can it be protected by the entry of a notice, but it can take effect as an overriding interest.

10.4 TERMINATION OF LEASES AND LICENCES

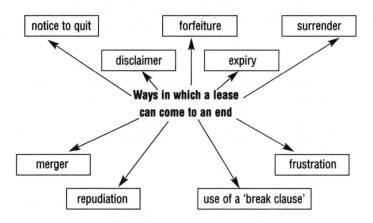

10.4.1 Ways of ending a lease

1. **Notice to quit** – either party can serve on the other a notice to quit which will indicate that they no longer wish the tenancy to continue.
   - The period of notice in a periodic tenancy is the equivalent period of each periodic term.
   - It is subject to the requirement that it must be given at least four weeks before the date on which it is to take effect.

2. **Forfeiture** – the lease may be forfeited if there is a breach of covenant. This is strictly regulated and is not available in cases of non-payment of rent until the landlord has formally demanded the rent.

- In other cases the landlord must serve a s146 LPA 1925 notice on the tenant.
- Amongst other things this notice must be in writing and must specify the breach and request the tenant to remedy this, as well as the tenant paying a sum in money to the landlord.
- The court has broad discretion to give relief against forfeiture for both non-payment of rent and other breaches.
- Relief will be granted where the arrears and costs are paid before trial.
- The court will also grant relief where the breach is not too serious, or there is a shortfall between the value of the property to be forfeited and the extent of the damage of the breach.
- Once forfeiture has been granted then the tenant becomes a trespasser.
- A sub-tenant's lease will also be forfeited unless they are granted relief by the court (s146(4)) and the court orders that the lease be vested in the sub-tenant.
- A landlord can only re-enter residential premises if they have an order from the court otherwise it is a criminal offence.
- The landlord must not have waived the right to forfeit by treating the tenancy as still continuing (e.g. accepting rent after the breach has taken place).

3. **Surrender** – a lease can be determined by the surrender of the interest of the tenant to his immediate landlord. This must be contained in a deed.

4. **Disclaimer** – this occurs in one of two ways:
   - either by the tenant clearly disclaiming his lease; or
   - where the liquidator of an insolvent company disclaims a lease owned by the company if it is seen to be unsaleable.

5. **Expiry** – a lease or tenancy ends automatically when the term expires.

6. **Merger** – if the tenant acquires the landlord's reversion while holding the tenancy, then the two interests become merged.

7. **Frustration** – if a supervening event has brought about a fundamental change of circumstances then the tenancy may be said to be frustrated (*National Carriers Ltd v Panalpina (Northern) Ltd* (1981) – closure of the only access road for 20 months of a ten-year lease did not entail frustration).

8. **Repudiation** – where there is a breach of a fundamental term then the courts may hold the agreement to be repudiated and the contract to be at an end (*Hussein v Mehlman* (1992)).

9. **A 'break clause'** – this can occur in commercial leases and it will allow either the landlord or the tenant to determine the lease on certain dates before the term expires.

10.5 THE REGULATION OF LEASES

10.5.1 Express covenants

1. There may be express obligations of both the landlord and the tenant in the lease.

2. The landlord may be bound in respect of repair, insurance and general maintenance of the premises.

3. The tenant may be bound by an obligation to pay rent or not to assign or sublet the premises.

10.5.2 Implied covenants

1. Where the lease is silent then common law or the lease will imply certain covenants into the agreement.

2. The landlord's implied covenants:
   i) quiet enjoyment
   ii) non-derogation from the grant
   iii) repair and fitness for habitation

3. Quiet enjoyment:
   - this means the landlord will not interfere with the tenant's enjoyment of the property (*Perera v Vandiyar* (1953));
   - it covers the prevention of direct and physical injury to the land, as well as less tangible interference caused by other tenants of the landlord (*Southwark LBC v Mills* (1999));

- this covenant is generally given a narrow construction;
- harassment of the tenant will be a breach of the covenant and will also be an offence under the Protection from Eviction Act 1977.
- Acts which merely inconvenience the tenant do not amount to a breach of quiet enjoyment (*Browne v Flower* (1917)).

4. Non-derogation from the grant:
- the landlord must not do anything that prevents the tenant from using the property for the purpose for which it was rented (*Harmer v Jumbil (Nigeria) Tin Areas Ltd* (1921));
- it may be a derogation from the grant if the landlord does not restrain a nuisance committed by other tenants of that landlord.

5. Repair and fitness for habitation:
- there is no general rule that a landlord must repair the property nor that it will be fit for occupation (*Southwark LBC v Mills* (1999));
- 'fraud apart, there is no rule against letting a tumbledown house', Erle CJ (*Robbins v Jones* (1863)).

6. The Common Law implied covenants for repair
- it is an implied condition that a furnished house will be reasonably fit for human habitation at the commencement of the term (*Smith v Marrable* (1843));
- it will not cover any deterioration of the premises during the currency of the lease;
- a landlord may have an implied contractual duty to take reasonable care to keep in repair certain facilities enjoyed by the tenant e.g. lifts, stairs and rubbish chutes (*Liverpool City Council v Irwin* (1977));
- there may also be limited liability which may extend to third parties as well as the tenant him/herself.

7. Statutory obligations of the landlord to keep the premises in good repair:
- ss8–10 Landlord and Tenant Act 1985 applies to houses let at low rent (set at such a low level that few properties qualify).

Implies that the premises are fit for human habitation both at the start of the tenancy and throughout the lease;

- ss11–16 Landlord and Tenant Act 1985 (only applies to leases of dwelling houses of less than 7 years) imply that the landlord will keep in good repair the structure and exterior, including drains, and also installations in the house for the supply of gas, water electricity and sanitation;
- the application may depend on where the property is situated (*Quick v Taff Ely BC* (1986));
- the landlord must be notified of the defect by the tenant before liability will arise (*O'Brien v Robinson* (1973)). Until recently, the courts have given disrepair a very limited definition. It does not involve improvement from the state of repair at the start of the tenancy.

8. Under the Defective Premises Act 1972 s4(1) the landlord has a statutory duty to take reasonable care to prevent personal injury or damage which may be caused by defects in the state of the demised premises.

10.5.3 The usual covenants

1. The landlord agrees to be bound to allow the tenant 'quiet enjoyment'.
2. The tenant agrees to:
   - pay rent;
   - pay rates and taxes;
   - to deliver up the premises in repair at the end of the term;
   - to allow the landlord to enter and view the premises at an agreed time if he is responsible for repair;
   - allow the landlord re-entry for non-payment of rent.

10.5.4 Remedies for breach of covenant

1. A landlord can:
   - seek forfeiture of the lease, but this right must be expressly reserved in the lease;

- the landlord has the option to waive the forfeiture or to enforce it;
- enforcement of forfeiture will be by way of re-entry. Possession proceedings are regarded as re-entry in residential premises where the landlord can only regain access by order of the court;
- the courts have the power to grant relief against forfeiture;
- seek an injunction and action for specific performance;
- sue for damages for breach of covenant.

2. A tenant can:

- sue for damages for breach of covenant;
- seek an order for specific performance;
- sue for distress for unpaid rent;
- take action for arrears of rent;
- use self-help and set-off (withholding future payments of rent), *Lee-Parker v Izzet* (1971).

10.6 THE ENFORCEMENT OF COVENANTS

10.6.1 Privity of contract and privity of estate

1. Covenants may be enforceable against assignees of the landlord or assignees of the tenant.

2. This will depend on whether there is privity of contract or privity of estate between the parties.

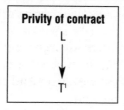

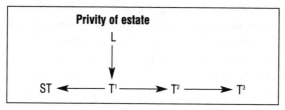

3. Before 1995 the landlord and the tenant would remain liable to each other for the whole term of the lease, even after assignment (*Hindcastle Ltd v Barbara Attenborough Associates Ltd* (1997)). This was because they had privity of contract and would remain liable on the terms of the contract.

4. Where the contract is validly assigned then the original landlord remains liable on the contract and T^1 will remain ultimately liable for unpaid rent but T^2 will be able to drop out of the picture when the tenancy is assigned to T^3.

5. If T sublets, then there will be privity of estate between T and ST (sub-tenant), but ST cannot sue L as there is no relationship of landlord and tenant between them. Likewise L cannot sue ST.

10.6.2 The running of covenants in leases

1. The benefit of L's covenants with T^1 can run at law to T^2. So too will the benefit of T's covenants with L.

2. The covenant must be shown to 'touch and concern' the land (*Spencer's Case* (1583)).

3. The burden of L's covenants with T^1 and T's covenants with L^1 will pass to L^2 if the covenants 'touch and concern the land' under (s141(benefit) and s142(burden) LPA 1925).

4. To 'touch and concern' the land means a covenant that relates to the land itself, or affects the landlord as landlord or tenant as tenant, e.g. a covenant to pay rent or to carry out repairs.

10.6.3 Tenancies under the old law

1. The running of covenants now depends on whether the tenancy was created before January 1 1996, referred to as an 'old tenancy'.
2. An old tenancy resulted in continuing liability for the tenant even after assignment.
3. These liabilities could even be increased after assignment as they could be varied by the assignee.
4. There is no privity of contract and privity of estate between the landlord and sub-tenant. The landlord can only sue the sub-tenant if:
   a) a restrictive covenant is contained in the head lease under the rule in *Tulk v Moxhay*;
   b) the lease to the tenant contained a forfeiture clause which, if enforced, will result in the sub-tenant's lease being terminated.

10.6.4 New tenancies under the Landlord and Tenant (Covenant) Act 1995

1. The Act removes liability from the tenant for tenant's covenants contained in the original lease, but he/she loses any right to enjoy landlord's covenants (L&T(C)Act 1995 s5).
2. T will remain liable for any breaches that occurred before the lease was assigned.
3. The principle of release cannot be varied by the parties (L&T(C)Act 1995).
4. There are two circumstances where there will be no release:
   - where the assignment was an 'excluded assignment' because it was in breach of covenant or operation of law;

- where release of T is postponed by the operation of an 'authorised guarantee agreement'.

5. An authorised guarantee agreement means that T guarantees the performance of tenant's covenants by T^2. It can only be made where there is an absolute covenant against assignment or when his or her consent is given subject to a condition that the tenant is to enter into an AGA.

6. Where the landlord assigns the reversion there is no automatic release from the covenants, but the landlord may give notice to the tenant and ask for release from the covenant (s6 L&T(C)Act 1995).

7. If the tenant refuses to release the landlord then he can apply to the court for release.

10.6.5 Provisions under the Landlord and Tenant (Covenants) Act 1995 applying to old tenancies

1. The original tenant cannot be required to pay rent or service charges owed by the present tenant unless the landlord has served a notice (a 'problem notice') informing him or her that any charge is due within six months of the date it becomes due.

2. Liability of the tenant cannot be increased by variation of the covenant.

3. The original tenant who has made such a payment of rent or other fixed charge may require the landlord to grant him or her an 'overriding lease' so that the original tenant becomes the immediate landlord of the current tenant.

CHAPTER 11

ADVERSE POSSESSION

Nature of rights under LRA 2002
- after 10 years the squatter can register
- notice is given to the paper title owner and others
- registration takes place if there is no response

OR in three other cases
- estoppel
- some other right in the land
- boundaries

Meaning
- No action shall be brought by any person to recover any land after 12 years – Limitation Act 1980 s15.
- Can be consecutive periods.

ADVERSE POSSESSION

Intention
Must show intention to treat land as ones own.

Factual possession
- Physical possession of the land, excluding all others.
- Not by a lease, licence or consent.
- Must be exercised openly.
- Enclosure is strong evidence, e.g. parking cars; fencing; grazing animals.

Recovery of land by paper title owner
- Must take legal proceedings.
- Can exercise self-help in limited circumstances.
- Can seek possession and interim possession order in county court.

11.1 THE MEANING OF ADVERSE POSSESSION

1. Adverse possession is based on the principle that if a paper title owner fails within a certain period to initiate the eviction of a squatter or trespasser from his land his title is lost.
2. No action shall be brought by any person to recover any land after the expiration of twelve years from the date on which the right of action accrued to him (LA 1980 s15).
3. Consecutive periods of adverse possession by different people may be added together (LA 1980 s15(1) *Mount Carmel Investments Ltd v Peter Thurlow Ltd* (1988)), provided there is no break between these periods.
4. LA 1980 s1(1) provides that the right of action starts to run when two elements are present:
   - paper title owners have given up possession of the land (either because they have been dispossessed or because they have discontinued their ownership);
   - squatters take possession of the land.
5. Squatters must prove:
   - that they have taken factual possession of the land;
   - that they have the necessary intention or *animus possidendi*.

11.2 FACTUAL POSSESSION

1. This involves physical possession of the land, which excludes all others including the paper title owner (*Powell v Macfarlane* (1977)).
2. Possession must be 'adverse' to the paper title owner, so it cannot be enjoyed by virtue of some lease, licence or consent from the paper title owner (*Colchester B.C. v Smith* (1992), *B.P. Properties v Buckler* (1987)).
3. Adverse possession need not be hostile to the paper title owner.
4. The factual possession of the land must be exercised openly and must not be concealed, to ensure that the paper title owner is given an opportunity to challenge the possession.

5. Squatters must prove that they have physical control over the property (*Bucks C.C. v Moran* (1990)).

6. 'Enclosure is the strongest possible evidence of adverse possession' – Cockburn CJ in *Seddon v Smith* (1877) (*Bucks C.C. v Moran* (1990) new lock and chain on the gate into the part of the land claimed by the squatter). Fencing is always good evidence of possession.

7. The paper title owner can no longer rely on the doctrine of implied licence (Limitation Act 1980 Schedule 1). This doctrine suggested that the owners could impliedly reserve themselves the right to return to the land without taking action to prevent the continued enjoyment of the property by the squatter.

8. Factual possession cannot be claimed on trivial acts of possession (*Tecbild Ltd v Chamberlain* (1969)).

9. What constitutes factual possession?
   - Parking of cars *Burns v Anthony* (1997);
   - Grazing of animals (*Treloar v Nute* (1976));
   - The erection of signs excluding trespassers (*Powell v Macfarlane* (1979) although no adverse possession was held in that case);
   - Shooting over a large area of land *Red House Farms v Catchpole* (1977).

11.3 THE INTENTION TO POSSESS

1. The squatter must show that he intended to treat the land as his own.

2. Hoffman J in *Bucks C.C. v Moran* (1990): 'the critical factor in adverse possession is not an intention to own but an intention to possess'.

3. Generally, intent is inferred from acts and is not based on declarations from the squatter himself.

11.4 THE NATURE OF THE RIGHTS IN ADVERSE POSSESSION

1. Once the squatter acquires rights in the property they are good against the world except anyone able to assert a better title.

2. Rights under the Limitation Act 1990 can be assigned *inter vivos* or passed under a will and, if the squatter dies intestate, the rights can pass to the next of kin. However there must be no evidence of a breach in possession.

11.5 RECOVERY OF POSSESSION BY THE PAPER TITLE OWNER

1. An action for recovery by the paper title owner must be brought before his right of recovery becomes statute-barred.

2. An action for possession requires the paper title owner to take legal proceedings and it is not enough to assert one's rights (*Mount Carmel Investments Ltd v Peter Thurlow Ltd* (1988)).

3. Adverse Possession can constitute a criminal offence under the Criminal Law Act 1977 s7(1) and the Criminal Justice and Public Order Act 1994 ss73 and 74 if a person, having entered as a trespasser, fails to leave premises on being required to do so.

4. Under civil law the paper title owner may exercise self-help at any stage before the squatter acquires possession of the property, but it must not itself constitute a criminal offence.

5. The paper title owner can also take an action for possession which can be available even where the names of the squatters are unknown. The documents can be served by fixing the relevant documents at the premises.

6. The County Court can also make an 'interim possession order' against an alleged trespasser on residential premises. Once made the order takes effect immediately and the hearing for a final possession order will be made during the next seven days.

11.6 MAIN CHANGES IN THE RULES ON ADVERSE POSSESSION INTRODUCED BY THE LRA 2002

1. The LRA 2002 introduced new rules in relation to the acquisition of rights by adverse possession over registered land.
2. There has been no change to the rules relating to unregistered land.
3. The Act does not change the rules concerning discontinuance and dispossession of land.

11.6.1 Registered Land

1. Under the new law adverse possession will not extinguish title to a registered estate however long it has been.
2. A squatter can apply to be registered as proprietor after ten years' adverse possession
3. The registered proprietor, any registered chargee and others interested in the land will be notified of the squatter's application
4. If the application is not opposed by any of those notified the squatter can be registered as proprietor
5. If any of those notified oppose the squatter's application it will be refused, unless the squatter can bring himself within one of the THREE exceptions:
   - estoppel
   - some other right in land
   - mistake over boundaries.
6. If the application is refused then the squatter can make a further application after 2 more years and the squatter will be registered as proprietor whether or not the registered proprietor objects.

11.6.2 Special Cases

1. Estoppel: the squatter must show that it was unconscionable to dispossess him or her; and that the circumstances are such that he or she ought to be registered as the proprietor;
   - it will be unconscionable if the registered proprietor encouraged or allowed the squatter to believe that he or she owned the land;
   - the squatter acted to his or her detriment to the knowledge of the proprietor;
   - it would be unconscionable for the proprietor to deny the squatter the rights which he or she believed he or she had;
   - the remedy can range from transfer of the property (*Pascoe v Turner* (1979)) to the grant of some right over the land *Crabb v Arun DC* (1976).
2. Some other right to the land. Examples could be:
   - the claimant is entitled under the will or intestacy of the deceased proprietor;
   - the claimant has contracted to buy the land and paid the purchase price but the legal estate was never transferred to the buyer.

   Claims under this provision will be relatively rare.
3. Mistake as to the boundary

   The squatter must prove:
   - there has been a period of adverse possession of at least ten years by the squatter or the squatter's predecessor in title ending on the date of the application;
   - for at least 10 years the squatter reasonably believed that the land to which the application relates belonged to him;
   - the estate to which the land relates was registered more than one year prior to the date of the application.

11.6.3 The effect of registration under the LRA 2002

1. Under the old law the registered proprietor held the land on bare trust for the squatter.
2. Under the new law there is no trust but automatic entitlement to be registered as the new proprietor as of right.
3. The squatter will take the land subject to the same estates, rights and interests that bound the previous proprietor.

INDEX